EDWARD WRIOTHESLEY RUSSELL

Design for Destiny

SCIENCE REVEALS THE SOUL

LONDON
NEVILLE SPEARMAN

First published in Great Britain
by Neville Spearman Limited
112 Whitfield Street, London W1P 6DP

Library of Congress Catalog Card Number
76–165309

SBN 85435 221 X

Set in 11-pt Baskerville, 1-pt leaded
by the Northumberland Press, Gateshead.
Bound by W. & J. Rawlinson, London

To my Wife

BARBARA

whose criticism has been invaluable
and encouragement unfailing

Contents

Foreword

This book is a synthesis and interpretation of the work of many minds. Its author's first duty, then, must be to acknowledge his debt and to express his gratitude to all those upon whose work this book is based. It 'stands on the shoulders of giants'.

To protect their reputations, however, it should be emphasized that none of the distinguished scientists quoted are in any way responsible for the use that has been made of their work; in fact, none of them have been aware of it. Some may be surprised because a reporter sees things differently from the specialist and is liable to give them a different emphasis. The author can only say that he has done his best to report their work accurately and to interpret its significance fairly.

A small map of a large country must omit much detail. There is no space for twists which, in reality, modify the apparent straightness of roads or rivers; many interesting byways, too, must be omitted. It is the same with this book which attempts to delineate a vast, unfamiliar territory in reasonable compass; there has been no space for many qualifications or details.

Early summaries of the evidence and conclusions were inflicted on a number of busy men and women in many walks of life in order to test their reactions. To all those who took the time to read these summaries and to offer valuable suggestions and criticisms—and also to encourage the completion of the investigation—the author owes more than he can say.

Thanks are also due to various individuals and publishers for permission to quote from copyright works.

Last—and most important—the author must record a

9

special debt of gratitude to his wife who has digested more drafts, ironed out more obscurities and caught more errors than he cares to remember. Despite this ordeal, somehow she has managed to remain cheerful and encouraging throughout the long—and sometimes painful—parturition of this book.

E. W. R.

Washington, D.C.

CHAPTER ONE

Perilous Questions

'The resistance to new ideas increases
by the square of their importance.'
—Russell's Law

1

What are we?

Why do we exist?

Is there a purpose in life?

If so, what is it and what should we do about it?

There is probably more uncertainty and disagreement about the answers to these questions in the present age than in any previous one. This has already caused us a lot of trouble and is likely to cause us a lot more unless we can find new and better answers on which more people can agree.

These questions are perilous because misleading or inadequate answers to them have had disastrous consequences: they have helped to precipitate two of the greatest plagues ever to afflict this planet—German militarism and Communism.

According to the distinguished historian, Barbara Tuchman,[1] German militarists, who roused their nation with their rantings about Germany's destiny as a superior race, indirectly drew their inspiration from Darwin's *Origin of Species* and used this theory to justify German attempts to dominate the world.

Many students of Communism agree[2] that it could not have appealed to so many people all over the world if the *idea* of Communism had not found an ideological vacuum into which it could flow with little resistance. It could not have made its phenomenal progress if the Churches and the philosophers had had better and more convincing answers to our four questions.

Civilization is still suffering from the consequences of German militarism; and every day of the week Communism costs us the lives of some of our finest men—and also enormous taxes for defence.

There might well have been more effective resistance to German militarism and also to the spread of Communism if the influence of the Churches had not been undermined by Darwin's answer to our first question. His theory that we have evolved from lower forms of animal life not only contradicted the Genesis story of the instant creation of Adam and Eve but also caused many people to doubt the whole teaching of the Churches and to adopt a purely materialistic explanation of human life. Darwin's theory, in fact, has encouraged many people to act irresponsibly—as even his disciples will occasionally admit[3]—because they seem to find the notion that their remote ancestors had primitive habits and swung by their tails from tree to tree a convenient excuse for almost anything.

Some authorities believe, too, that some of the present world-wide student unrest is partly due to the fact that many of the younger generation see no purpose in life—can find no satisfying answers to our third and fourth questions. Mr. Nelson A. Rockefeller, indeed, has gone so far as to say that if future American policy is to be effective, we must find some way to give life meaning.[4]

On his return from Europe, President Nixon told a Press Conference (March 4, 1969) that the chief reason for world-wide student unrest is that the younger generation lacks 'a sense of purpose in life' and that 'we must try to give it to them'.

'We don't yet know how to do this,' the President said, 'but we are working on it.'

Even some Communists feel the same need. Some years ago, for instance, Dr. Adam Schaff, Poland's leading Marxist philosopher, reproached Communist philosophers for neglecting questions concerning 'the meaning of life' and wrote that Communism stands to lose 'the struggle for the mind of man' unless its philosophy comes to grips with the problem of the human individual and his fate.[5]

With their reduced influence, the Churches can no longer satisfy as many people as they used to do with their answers to our questions. Nor can they exercise as much discipline as formerly, nor keep so many people more or less in line with promises of 'heaven' or threats of 'hell'—which may have something to do with the increasing crime and lawlessness of this age. This, of course, is not all Darwin's fault: mass-entertainment has made 'heaven' less alluring while science and mass-education have made 'hell' less convincing.

When the Churches' congregations can enjoy all the top TV entertainers and exciting news-programmes with the flip of a switch, the promised diversions of 'heaven' in some indefinite place and future may easily seem too tame to worry about. 'Eternal bliss', singing hymns of praise or even 'casting down our brassy crowns around a glassy sea' (as an old hymn suggests) cannot have the same appeal as the World Series, the top-rating shows or even the news-commentators. If, in fact, the supposed entertainments of 'heaven' were available for TV it is improbable that they would find a sponsor. Many people, therefore, are more likely to worry about making the next monthly payment on their large-screen, colour TV than about making much effort to qualify for 'heaven'.

Meanwhile, mass-education and the mass-media have engendered more respect for science than for religion; and science—officially, at least—does not recognize 'hell', or even a future existence. Old-fashioned notions of hell-fire and a Day of Judgement, therefore, make no impression on those who believe that science knows everything.

Others, who may have some vague belief in an after-life with rewards and punishments, read almost daily newspaper accounts of the uncertainties, delays, loopholes and quibbles of human criminal justice, especially in the United States. When they see how easy it is to circumvent the laws of this world, they may well feel—if only subconsciously—that the laws of the next must be even easier to evade and that there is no need to worry about a streamlined Judgement Day with swift and certain penalties. They may well expect that the Merciful and Loving Judge promised by the Churches will be even more lenient—and even more receptive to some quibble advanced by a favourite Saint as counsel for the defence—than the Supreme Court of the United States.

To regain their lost authority, the Churches need a more enticing 'heaven' and a more credible 'hell'. And in looking for the answers to our four questions we shall find something that may help them.

Though the Churches no longer enjoy their former influence—thanks to Darwin, science and the devaluation of 'heaven' and 'hell'—paradoxically they still retain vast and, sometimes, growing memberships. According to the eminent theologian, Dr. Paul Tillich—writing some years ago—the current interest in religion was due to the fact that man has lost 'the dimension in depth'. By this he meant that man has 'lost an answer to the question: "What is the meaning of life? Where do we come from, where do we go to? What shall we do, what should we become, in the short stretch between birth and death?" . . . And the resurgence of religion is nothing but a desperate and mostly futile attempt to regain what has been lost.'[6]

This distinguished authority not only recognized the widespread need to find better answers to our four questions but also realized that present attempts to do so are 'mostly futile'.

Even those who are lucky enough to enjoy a religious faith which answers these questions to their own satisfaction may feel that the more we can find out about our existence the better. For we move around on the surface of an insignificant planet in bodies which are more trouble and expense to house, fuel and service than any automobile. So it makes sense to find out all we can about these remarkable vehicles and also about any traffic-rules which may govern their use.

It is also useful to know where we are heading and interesting to try to find out what happens after our bodies wear out and have to be junked by the undertaker.

Many busy people, of course, are quite happy to wait till that moment to find out unless, perhaps, they lose someone they love. Then they may want to know whether they will meet him or her in another existence and, if so, how they will find each other and what that existence will be like.

For personal as well as public reasons, then, the reader may

14

agree that it is worthwhile to search for some clues to better answers to these four questions.

2

Such a search is now possible because certain modern discoveries at last offer some entirely new clues to better answers. These have so far escaped the attention of our philosophers and clergy, partly because they have only become available in the past thirty years and partly because they are scattered, little-known and—in some cases—as unpopular among the pundits as a roaring drunk at a concert of chamber-music.

From our point of view this is a great advantage. For we are free to follow a new trail of our own and need not bother to retrace the well-worn trails of theology or philosophy, with their often-indecypherable blazes of dogma, metaphysics or technical jargon. There is no need, too, to be as solemn on our trail as most philosophers and clergy, who have overlooked the obvious fact that the Creator must have a—literally— 'divine sense of humour'. One has only to look at such products of creation as, say, a mandrill—cheerfully flaunting a *derriere* in 'Glorious Technicolor'—or a Pekinese or, for that matter, the human race to be certain that humour played a large part in the origin of the creatures that live on this planet. Besides, how could *we* possess any sense of humour at all if our Creator did not possess an infinitely better one?

There is no need, therefore, to approach the mysteries of life with the attitude of a certain terrified African chief from what would now be called an 'emerging nation'. In the dark days before it had emerged, its chief went to London to pay his respects to Queen Victoria, wriggled on his king-size belly for the entire length of the Throne Room at Buckingham Palace and lay prostrate and perspiring at Her Majesty's feet. This placed almost as great a strain on the solemnity of the Queen as some of our clergy must impose on the gravity of the Creator.

Still less need we crawl on our bellies through the Throne Rooms of Science, though Science, of course, is wonderful. It has given us such delights as hydrogen bombs, wonder-drugs, colour TV and deodorants 'proved by scientific test' to be effective on the hottest dance-floor and not to irritate the most sensitive skin. (What fun some 'scientists' must have!) In spite of this, however, we must always remember that Science does not know everything and that there are many important subjects quite beyond the scope of its 'disciplines', which, in fact, tend to shackle most scientists and to make them narrow in their outlook. 'An expert is a man who knows nothing else'—as Guy Thorne put it.

We must recognize, too, that there are scientists and 'scientists'. Without name-dropping, this reporter can say that he has been privileged to know personally some of the great scientists of this age. He has therefore learned to distinguish between the true scientist and the mere technician—the mass-production-model 'scientist' churned out by the education industry.

A really great scientist can usually be identified by an intellectual modesty and an ever-open mind—which is no coincidence as Nature is reluctant to reveal her major secrets to those who approach her arrogantly. The run-of-the-mill 'scientist', by contrast, too often feels that a degree confers omniscience, even on subjects which were never included in the curriculum. And such is the present prestige of Science as a whole, many naïve people are prepared to accept the views of any 'scientist' on any subject—from foreign policy to the prospects of immortality.

As we shall see, this book is made possible by the work of true scientists; and we shall find ourselves deeply in their debt. But we owe no obeisance to the deacons of science who intone the current dogma of the hierarchy.

Any reader, however, who is afraid to lose his scientific virginity, is advised to read no further and to return this book to the library—preferably in a plain wrapper because one never knows whom one may meet in libraries. To be seen openly carrying this book might start rumours among colleagues—particularly those anxious to get his job—that the bearer is not 'sound' or even trying to 'rock the boat'. And, if he read beyond this point, he might risk impregnation with heretical ideas, anathema to the Scientific Priesthood.

In either case, he might well jeopardize, if not his job, at least his next research-grant. And he might also risk permanent exclusion from those innumerable Conferences About Nothing Much which—thanks to the Foundations and the taxpayer—are such an enjoyable feature of modern scientific life.

This friendly warning is prompted by the puerile and vindictive attitude of the Scientific Establishment towards Dr. Immanuel Velikovsky, author of the famous book, *Worlds in Collision.*[7] In this scholarly work—as some readers will remember—Dr. Velikovsky advanced theories which infuriated some 'scientists' because they conflicted with what they had been taught and were teaching—especially Darwin's Theory. These emotional pedagogues completely lost their heads and not only vilified and misquoted Dr. Velikovsky but also tried their utmost to get his book suppressed. They brought every kind of pressure on anyone who supported him, successfully intimidated a famous publisher and got at least one man fired from his job.[8]

Fortunately, they did not silence Dr. Velikovsky, who has since published other successful books (with another publisher). And the pedagogues have been made to look even more foolish by fresh evidence that has become available to support Dr. Velikovsky's theories. But this attempted book-burning by American 'scientists' shows the professional risks run by anyone who owes his job to the Scientific Establishment if he so much as casts a lustful eye on the harlots of scientific heresy.

3

Readers who can afford to ignore this warning and who are game to continue may like to know what to expect:

This book is a former newspaper-reporter's report, with some 'news-interpretation'. This reporter has dug up some discoveries and phenomena which are like the individual pieces of a jig-saw puzzle. When these pieces are fitted together, collectively they form a significant picture which suggests some answers to our four questions.

With the present limitations of our knowledge—and of the human mind—it would be arrogant to promise and foolish to expect complete and final answers to the four questions.

The answers that we shall find are approximate—some of them not more than 'educated guesses'. But the need for some better answers than we have had up till now is so urgent that something imperfect or approximate is surely better than nothing at all.

For many years we have been living in an 'ideological emergency'—in a war of ideas; and, in emergencies, one cannot afford to wait for perfection. During World War II, for instance, the British had to 'freeze' the design of certain types of radar, though they knew they could be improved, in order to get them into production and operational use.

There are, of course, no instant answers to our questions— the pieces in the puzzle will take a little time to fit together. But this will take no longer—and be no harder—than piecing together the clues in a good mystery story. As far as possible technical terms will be avoided, though we shall find it necessary to invent some of our own to describe some things which we shall find and for which, at present, no terms exist. Every effort, too, will be made to eliminate jargon which—too often in these days—is either a symptom of illiteracy, a disguise for uncertainty or just plain pomposity.

We shall have to consider certain phenomena which are not yet recognized—and are usually ridiculed—by the pundits. But *all of these can be verified by the reader himself*, if he has an open mind and is willing to take the same amount of time and trouble as this reporter

For the benefit of readers who want further details—or who want to check up—references have been given, grouped by chapters, at the end of this book. These are working references, all of them relevant and, it is hoped, interesting and useful. The list has not been 'padded', after the current academic fashion, with numerous and mainly-irrelevant references—apparently intended either to show how well-read the author is or else to dope the reader into a state of bemused credulity.

When certain interpretations are made or deductions suggested, the reader must judge for himself whether these seem reasonable and make sense. For this is really a 'do-it-yourself' book. It only aims to suggest ideas which, if he wishes, the reader himself can improve and adapt to his own use, in much the same way as the hobbyist will improve on the design for a book-shelf or kitchen-cabinet. Like the writers of the 'do-it-yourself' books, this reporter has nothing to sell—no desire to convert—and hopes that the reader himself can develop the ideas suggested in this book.

There is plenty of room for development. As we follow the trail we shall notice some intriguing side-trails which would take too long to explore but to which the reader may like to return in the future.

4

As this book is not a mystery-story and its aim, in fact, is to remove as much mystery as possible, there is no need to keep the impatient reader in suspense. Though it will take time to fit together all the pieces in the picture, it is possible to give a brief preview of the answers to the four questions which the evidence will suggest.

In answer to the first question: *What are we?* we shall find that we are much more than mere chemical machines— much more than 'what our genes make us' as some current biological fantasies suggest. Far from being the chance products of improbable chemistry, we shall find that we depend for our very existence and individual identity on intangible, organizing factors which are the opposite of chance. As the product of organization, human life is no accident and has purpose.

As this is written, that magical, double-helical molecule, deoxyribonucleic acid—affectionately known as DNA—is the latest craze, almost as fashionable as Darwin's Theory at the height of its popularity. Uncritical enthusiasts believe that DNA can explain everything—from a Beethoven to a bunion —and that it is the 'Master Key to the Secret of Life'. If it has not happened already, we shall soon see a murderer released from gaol to continue murdering because some biological 'expert' has convinced the Court that the poor fellow's double-helix merely got a bit tangled, which was not his fault.

Some biologists, it is true, believe that DNA-filled genes do not determine traits but merely govern the responses of the person to 'environmental stimuli'. In other words they think that genes themselves do not produce a bunion or Beethoven but make an individual bunion-prone or music-prone. How 'environmental stimuli' then produce a bunion or a musical genius is not explained.

As we shall see, DNA is only one of the factors that make us what we are and by no means the most important one, even though the discovery that the molecule is formed as a double helix is hailed as the greatest biological 'breakthrough' of the age. And we shall leave the biologists to scramble on to the DNA band-wagon while, in the next chapter, we consider a far greater 'breakthrough', made over thirty years ago, which most biologists have overlooked.

To the next question: *Why do we exist?* it is tempting—in this Age of the Larger Lunacies—to answer that we must exist for the amusement of our Creator who, perhaps, 'keeps' the human race for much the same reasons that we keep pets. And, seriously, if we credit the Creator with a sense of humour, we cannot exclude that as at least a part of the explanation of our existence. There is, however, plenty of evidence that Nature is an enthusiastic experimenter and it is safe to deduce that the development of the human race is one of her more important experiments.

(Incidentally, until we can consider Who or What started the Universe and controls it, it is probably simpler to use the term 'Nature' to describe the creative, organizing force behind life.)

Nature's great experiment with the human race is not only more important but also much riskier than some of her earlier experiments with, say, dinosaurs or dodos, because man has more ability and free-will than such creatures. They merely failed to survive in the struggle for existence and, as far as we know, their extinction did not upset any other experiments. But man now has the ability and the means to wreck all Nature's experiments on this planet by blowing it up.

So Nature seems to have taken a calculated risk with man by giving him a certain degree of control of her most daring experiment. If we can only guess at her motives, at least we can deduce that she regards the development of the human race as sufficiently interesting or important to be willing to risk the destruction of all her other experiments on this planet.

What part does Nature expect man to play in her experiment? What does she hope he will do with the free-will she allows him? This brings us to our third and fourth questions: *Is there a purpose in life? If so, what is it and what should we do about it?*

We shall find that there is a purpose in life which—as far as we are concerned—is *to develop the individual character and personality by experience, whether the experience be pleasant or unpleasant.* We shall also find that everything we can achieve in this way is not wasted because memory—the essence of personality and the storehouse of experience—*is conserved for our use in future existences.* In other words our personalities and our memories are not extinguished by death.

Since the individual is important in Nature's experiment, so is his freedom because, obviously, he cannot develop his individuality without as much freedom as possible. We shall find, then, that dictators and others who like needlessly to restrict the freedom of the individual are going against Nature's plan which—as any farmer could tell them—eventually leads to trouble.

There is another side, of course, to the coin of freedom. Since the individual and his freedom are a part of Nature's experiment, the individual is personally responsible for what he does with what Nature has given him. And although some modern excuses for misusing freedom may impress judges and juries, we shall find that they cannot influence Nature.

For Nature is no 'bleeding-heart'—she sometimes seems even more ruthless than a Himmler—and is not so naïve as to conduct her experiments without some controls. We can see that some checks on man's conduct are necessary because the gross misuse of personal freedom by one individual—say, a Stalin, a Hitler or a Mafia chieftain—can destroy the opportunity of many other individuals to take part in Nature's experiment. So we shall find that Nature does arrange *personal* penalties for the individual who misuses his freedom and that these penalties cannot be evaded. With all eternity to work with, however, she is in no hurry and the eternal personality may not—and often does not—suffer any penalties

21

in the *present* existence. This explains the Psalmist's lament that 'the wicked flourish like the green bay tree' and why—in modern parlance—so many crooks seem to 'get away with murder'.

If she wishes, however, Nature can impose instant penalties because she never graduated from Law School or learned the delaying, make-work practices invented by our lawyers' Trade Unions.

5

That is merely a brief summary—for the impatient reader—of only some of the things we shall discover; and readers who find these brief, bald statements hard to swallow are asked to reserve judgement until they have considered the evidence and reasoning on which they are based.

They are also asked to remember that if the answers we are looking for are to be any use, *they will have to be new and unorthodox*, because the old orthodox answers have had unfortunate consequences, as we have seen. And inevitably, the new and unorthodox often seem startling, until we get used to them. Indeed, new ideas of any sort are far less welcome than illegitimate babies—and far harder to put out to adoption.

Contrary to popular superstition that new ideas receive a rapturous reception in this 'age of progress', the fact is that they are just as unpopular as they were in the Dark Ages—more so, perhaps, if they encroach on today's academic preserves, as Dr. Velikovsky's did. As Dr. Kettering, the great inventor is said to have remarked: 'People are all in favour of new ideas, provided they are exactly like the old ones.'

We must expect, then to disturb—and perhaps to be disturbed—by some of the things we shall find. We must be prepared, when necessary, to tread on some professional corns, to question some vested interests and to face the inevitable howls of pain or protest.

But that, surely, is a small price to pay if we can find some better answers to our four perilous—and pressing—questions.

CHAPTER TWO

Breakthrough

It's a very odd thing—
As odd as can be—
That whatever Miss T eats
Turns into Miss T.
—*Walter de la Mare*[1]

1

One of the most significant—and least-known—discoveries of recent times is the extent to which the material of the human body is constantly destroyed and renewed. The modern biological tool of 'tagged elements' has revealed that the components of our bodies are ceaselessly torn apart and reconstructed with fresh material derived from our food.

If Mr. de la Mare had realized how much Miss T, of the verse quoted above, was not only growing but also changing in substance he would have thought it even odder. For, with a poet's perception, he marvelled at a mystery that most of us take for granted: how is all the varied food consumed by Miss T—candy, roast-turkey and cranberry-sauce or that horrific diet of modern youth, peanut-butter and jelly—how is all this converted into the many kinds of molecules which Miss T needs not only to grow but also to replace all the material of her body that is destroyed every day?

It has long been known, of course, that we constantly renew our skin, hair and blood. But, until some biochemists learned how to introduce radio-active elements into the body, which can be photographed after they have been incorporated in the body-cells, nobody realized that most, if not all, of us is being perpetually renewed.

Whether or not we accept the idea of reincarnation, the fact is that—literally—we have often been 'reincarnated' in

23

our present lifetime, when most of the materials of our bodies and brains have been replaced with fresh material.

All the protein of which we are so largely composed is frequently renewed. This, of course, does not happen suddenly, but continuously. Liver and serum proteins are turned over every ten days and the proteins of the lungs, brain, skin and principal muscles are turned over every 158 days. Even bone, once thought to be permanent, is constantly replaced with fresh material. Only the *design* of our bodies, changing slightly with growth or age, remains constant. As the distinguished British authority, Sir Charles Dodds, once put it graphically: [2]

'In the case of man the total turnover of protein occurred in about 80 days, while the liver and serum proteins were turned over in 10 days and the lung, brain, bone, skin and principal muscle in 158 days. . . .

'When one contrasts the great complexity of the protein molecule with the fact that millions of these substances are constantly being built up and disintegrated in the human body, and moreover rebuilt to precisely the same structure, one cannot help but speculate about the controlling mechanism. *It is a rather terrifying thought that the whole of the protein in the human body is replaced in roughly 160 days*, and at the present time, we can only speculate on the mechanism controlling this elaborate resynthesis, where even a single amino-acid must not be out of place if the hormone is to have its activity or the antibody its potency.' (Our italics.)

It is significant that Sir Charles implied that there must be a 'mechanism' to 'control this elaborate re-synthesis'; he did not suggest that these complex molecules can rebuild themselves.

But the modern technique of using 'labelled' isotopes as 'tracer' molecules leaves no doubt that this 'elaborate re-synthesis' is always going on. We are constantly changing the molecules of our bodies—this year's molecules are not the same as last year's, even though we look and feel the same. This process of renewal is continuous. Every atom and molecule in

our tissues is constantly swapping materials with its surround-
ings. And after about six months we will have had a complete
turnover of material, with new material made out of our food
and drink and the air we breathe.

We also renew our cells. All the living cells and bacteria
in our bodies are really tiny factories which convert our food
into energy and new materials needed by the body and ex-
crete the waste products. These cells, however, are constantly scrapped and replaced. According to the well-known
American biologist, Dr. Hudson Hoagland, there are 60,000
billion cells in the human body and of these 500 billion
cells of some types *die every day* and are replaced by new
ones.[3]

Even bone is now known to have a turnover of material
far more extensive than was previously supposed, according
to scientists of the National Institutes of Health, Bethesda,
Md.[4]

'Bone, once thought to be completely inert, actually
wears out and is replaced constantly in the normal human
skeleton. This turnover is similar to the continual replacement of the body's skin.'

Our brains and nervous systems are no exception to this
general rule of constant renewal of material:

Anyone who has had first-aid training knows how much
the brain depends on oxygen and for how few minutes it can
last without it. As Sir Charles Sherrington, the famous physio-
logist, once wrote:[5]

'There is . . . the circulation of the blood always going forward. Where each small artery plunges into the brain, a
little whirlpool of blood is visible. This brings home to us
how very eagerly the brain breathes. *The brain is, of course,
a corporeal thing and composed like other body organs of
just physico-chemical stuff, which breaks down finally into
waste products.*' (Our italics.)

In short, the bits and pieces of which our brains and bodies are made up are constantly being torn apart and put together again with new material but in the same form. 'Whatever Miss T eats' turns not only into Miss T but into a *rebuilt* Miss T.

2

As another authority puts it: [6]

'. . . some results of modern biochemistry . . . suggest that *all constituents of living matter, whether functional or structural, are in a steady state of rapid flux.*' (Our italics.)

Why is all this rebuilding necessary? Three other authorities suggest an explanation: [7]

'The picture one perceives is of a ceaseless deamination and reamination of most amino acids.

'It might seem that this dynamic equilibrium is a great waste of energy, that it would be more economical on the part of living matter to allow its proteins, fat and other constituents to remain fixed in position. Probably this idea of "rest" is a false one. Actually, the molecules with which the body deals are, of necessity, so complex that they lack sufficient inherent stability to "rest". . . . Their instability is such that they are forever falling apart and any device whereby they are put together again at an equivalent rate can allow the body to make use of their tremendously complex structure.'

Our bodies, in other words, have to have molecules so complex that they are highly unstable and 'forever falling apart'. How could such molecules possibly *rebuild themselves*? How could the body use them unless it possessed some 'mechanism' to rebuild them exactly as they were before?

This seems even more obvious when we remember that the body is largely composed of liquids in constant circulation and that it can use food of great variety which, by some unimaginable chemistry, is converted into an even greater variety of molecules, *at the right time and in the right places.*

Through all this constant change, however, the body as a whole is amazingly stable. When we meet a friend we have not seen for six months, we recognize him immediately, even though all the protein that makes up his face has been changed and there is not one molecule in it that was there when we last saw him.

As we get older, it is true, our appearance changes but in most of us the changes are slow and our general appearance remains surprisingly constant through adult life.

Healthy bodies, too, can retain their form and stability under all kinds of conditions and under all kinds of stress— as two World Wars have shown. Moreover, when necessary they can produce special substances like antibodies to fight infection, scar-tissues to close wounds or extra adrenalin for emergencies.

Our bodies, then, must possess a remarkable 'mechanism' not only to maintain their form through ceaseless changes of material but also to ensure their stability in many varied conditions and emergencies.

This 'mechanism' has now been discovered, though the news has not yet penetrated most scientific circles. It has not only been discovered but carefully studied over the past thirty years. This is an authentic 'breakthrough' and perhaps the most important single contribution to medicine and biology of this age. For this is a *basic* discovery of the highest significance and with many potential applications in nearly every branch of medicine and biology.

3

In brief, this great discovery is that all living forms—whether they be the human body, animals, trees, plants or lower forms of life—possess, and are controlled, by electromagnetic fields. These are the organizing 'mechanisms' that keep all living forms in shape and that build, maintain and repair them through constant changes of material.

This is no longer just a theory. These electromagnetic 'fields of life' have been measured and mapped with great precision by modern instruments. And many thousands of experiments have not only confirmed their existence but also have shown many of the things that they do.

Credit for this discovery is entirely due to Dr. Harold Saxton Burr and Dr. F. S. C. Northrop, both of Yale. As long ago as 1935, they first published their 'Electrodynamic Theory of Life'.[8] Since then, in countless experiments, with special instruments and techniques, Dr. Burr, Dr. Northrop and their associates have not only confirmed their theory beyond all reasonable doubt but also have learned a lot about the 'fields of life' and how they behave.

Dr. Burr and his colleagues have published innumerable papers on the subject but most of these have appeared in scientific journals with a limited circulation.[9] This and also their extremely modest approach to their discovery partly explain why it has not received the attention it deserves.*

In one way, Dr. Burr and his associates are lucky that their important discoveries have merely been ignored. For, as history shows, earlier pioneers in the field of medicine were actively defamed and persecuted. Pasteur, for instance, was given a rough time by his professional colleagues and Lister made himself most unpopular by suggesting that germs are a Bad Thing. And it is reported that when one of Lister's French students hurried back to France to spread the glad news he was promptly lynched

So far—it is pleasant to report—Dr. Burr has escaped these perils of the pioneer and is peacefully retired as the E. K. Hunt Professor of Anatomy, Emeritus, of the Yale University School of Medicine.

It is only fair to say, however, that fields are elusive things and hard to visualize. They cannot be seen and can only be detected by their effects on instruments or objects. And it is only in recent times that fields, rather than particles, have become fashionable in physics.

Physicists define a field something like this: when some-

---

* For much of the following description of electrodynamic fields the author is indebted to Dr. Burr, who generously allowed him to read the MS of his forthcoming book. This important work—the first comprehensive description of Dr. Burr's great discovery—will be published in the near future by Neville Spearman Ltd.

thing occurs somewhere in space because something else happened somewhere else in space, with no visible means by which the cause produced the effect, the two events are connected by a 'field'. So there is some excuse for biologists who feel safer on the solid ground of chemistry. You can see and hold a test-tube but you cannot do that with a field.

Though we cannot see or feel the fields which control our bodies, a rough analogy may help to visualize them: the familiar school experiment with a magnet and iron filings. As everyone knows, when we sprinkle a card with iron filings and hold it over an ordinary magnet, the filings will arrange themselves in a pattern that represents the 'lines of force' of the magnet's field. And though we can change the filings as often as we like, each set of filings will always assume the same pattern.

That is an extremely crude illustration of the way in which the 'fields of life' keep the changing atoms, molecules, and cells in the same pattern. The human electromagnetic field, of course, is infinitely more complicated than an ordinary magnetic field because it contains many local or 'sub-fields' of the atoms, molecules, cells and organs which, to some extent, interact with it. Despite this 'feed-back' from the sub-fields there is plenty of evidence that the overall field of the body is primary and controls its component fields.

Though the human fields are complicated and all the details of them are not yet known, there is no mystery about measuring them. This is done with any good modern vacuum-tube voltmeter of such high resistance—at least ten megohms—that it draws virtually no current from the body and therefore does not affect the voltage patterns in the field which are being measured. These are d.c. potentials and have nothing to do with brain-waves or with the currents measured by an electrocardiograph. Some scientists affect to deny the reality of any phenomenon they cannot measure (one wonders how they managed to fall in love with their wives) and the validity of any experiment that is not repeatable. The blessed word 'repeatable', in fact, occurs as often in the liturgy of science as 'Amen' in the prayer books.

These arbitrary conditions are fully met by the 'fields of life'. They can be measured with great accuracy, even in such tiny living forms as seeds; and experiments are repeatable. Even by the most pedantic, therefore, the 'fields of life' can be considered a scientifically-respectable phenomenon, eligible one day for the *imprimatur* of the hierarchy. When that will be will depend on how long it takes biochemists to lose their enthusiasm for present fashions.

Meanwhile, as we shall consider them further, it will be convenient to coin a short name for the electromagnetic (or 'electrodynamic'), organizing fields, which are found in all living forms—that is, for the 'fields of life'. As, oddly enough, even Dr. Burr himself has not yet given them a short title, we must take it upon ourselves to call them '*L-fields*'.

4

Dr. Burr and his colleagues devoted over thirty years to painstaking experiments which not only confirmed the existence of L-fields in all forms of life—from men to rabbits, from trees to slime moulds—but also revealed many of their properties. This long and assiduous research, however, did include some historic and exciting moments:

After three years had been spent on developing instruments sufficiently sensitive and stable accurately to measure the voltages in the L-fields, one of the earliest experiments was to measure the fields of male and female volunteers over a long period of time. Voltage-gradients in the female L-field, in particular, were carefully measured and recorded, day after day, week after week and month after month.

These records revealed a substantial voltage-rise, lasting about 24 hours, once a month in the L-fields of most women; and it was found from their medical records that these rises occurred about the middle of the menstrual cycle. This, of course, suggested that ovulation is associated with a rise in voltage in the female L-field and—even more important— that a change in the voltage-gradient accompanies a fundamental biological activity.[10]

This exciting confirmation not only of the Field Theory but also of the importance of the L-field inspired the pioneers to make further experiments:

They hit on the idea of using a female rabbit because it is

known that rabbits ovulate about nine hours after stimulation of the cervix. So a rabbit was stimulated and nine hours later was anaesthetized. Its abdomen was then opened and one electrode, connected to the voltmeter, was placed close to the ovary and the other electrode was attached to the animal's body. While the ovary was continuously observed with a microscope, the changing voltages were recorded on a recording galvanometer.

Suddenly it happened, to the awe and delight of the scientists: at the moment when—through the microscope—they saw the follicle rupture and the egg released there was a sharp change in the voltage on the recorder.[11]

Shortly after this, a young woman had to have an operation and volunteered to let this be done when her electrical records indicated that ovulation was imminent. When her voltage-gradients started to rise, she was taken to the operating room and an ovary uncovered. A recently-ruptured follicle was observed—which confirmed the findings in the rabbit.[12]

These experiments were historic in two ways. They afforded dramatic evidence of the part played by L-fields in biology. And, for the first time, they showed that the moment of ovulation can accurately be determined electrically.

This remarkable discovery has great practical implications. For numerous measurements of female L-fields have revealed that some women may ovulate over the entire menstrual cycle, that ovulation may occur without menstruation and menses without ovulation. The potential importance of this knowledge to gynaecology, family-planning and birth-control is obvious. It also helps to explain why the 'rhythm method' of birth-control is inadequate.

A patient of Dr. Burr's, a married woman, made good use of this discovery. For years she and her husband had longed in vain to have children. So, over a period of many weeks, she made regular visits to Dr. Burr's laboratory and measured the voltages in her own L-field with his instruments. When, one day, she saw them rising rapidly she knew that ovulation was imminent and went to her husband. A longed-for—and much loved—child was the happy result of this application of Dr. Burr's discovery.[13]

It was also applied by the distinguished obstetrician and

gynaecologist, Dr. Louis Langman, to the problem of timing artificial insemination and proved more successful for this purpose than other methods of timing ovulation.[14]

Another dramatic and significant milestone in this research was the discovery that abnormal voltage-gradients in the L-field can reveal the presence of abnormal physical conditions.[15]

In the wards of New York's Bellvue Hospital, Dr. Langman and his assistant examined about a thousand female patients with Dr. Burr's instruments, the electrodes being placed on the cervix and the ventral abdominal wall. In 102 cases, the abnormal voltage-gradient suggested the existence of malignancy. Subsequent surgery confirmed that malignancy *did* exist in no less than 95 of the 102 women.

If or when the medical historians study the work of Dr. Burr and his associates they will note April 24, 1948, as an important date in the history of medicine. For it was on this day that the *effect of hypnosis on the L-field* was first observed and recorded by Dr. Leonard J. Ravitz, Jr.

To the astonishment of those present, a continuously-recording voltmeter showed changes in the voltage-gradient of the L-field of a patient as he sank deeper and deeper into hypnosis. For the first time in history it was possible to measure the *depth of hypnosis* objectively with a voltmeter.[16]

For our investigation this is a most important clue, as we shall see shortly: *mind* can produce measurable electrical changes in the L-field.

For obvious reasons men and women cannot be kept wired up to voltmeters for months and years. But trees can be because they do not move about. For many years, therefore, Dr. Burr kept recording voltmeters connected to a maple tree in New Haven and to a magnificent old elm in Old Lyme, Connecticut.[17] Over the years measurements of the L-fields of these trees revealed voltage changes not only between day and night but also with storms, lunar cycles and sun-spot variations. If—as seems probable—similar variations in the human L-field can be established, this will be important not only in the study of health and behaviour but also of physical problems which may arise in space exploration.

5

In addition to these dramatic discoveries the long years of research produced other striking and significant findings with useful practical implications:

The L-field of the body, for instance, changes when wounds are healing. This offers a simple way to measure the *rate* of healing, particularly useful in the case of the internal wounds from operations.[18]

Measurement of changes in the human L-field can reveal not only the effects of hypnosis but also of sleep and of drugs —another tool for medicine.[19]

Changes in the voltage-patterns of L-fields have been found in patients suffering from such varied symptoms as schizophrenia, fear or ulcers. This may offer a new diagnostic tool.

Dr. Ravitz has found that mentally-unstable people display erratic voltage-patterns *before* there are any obvious symptoms. This will make it possible for the Armed Forces and industrial recruiters to weed out—by objective electronic means—unsuitable personnel before time and money are wasted on training them for duties for which they are psychologically unsuited.

L-field measurements of patients in mental hospitals can offer a new and entirely objective method of finding out whether a patient is well enough to be discharged. When this method is adopted the public will be protected from dangerous lunatics turned loose too soon and the taxpayers will be saved the expense of maintaining patients who could safely be released.

L-field measurements can also be useful to healthy men and women because—when measured over a period of a few weeks—the measurements show cyclical rises and falls of voltage, which can be plotted in steady curves. These 'peaks and valleys' of the voltage-curves indicate the times when the individual is at his best and the times when his efficiency and vitality are low. As the curves of healthy men and women are steady and regular over long periods they can be projected ahead and used to *predict* 'highs' and 'lows' weeks in advance.

This knowledge could be of great value to those engaged in hazardous occupations, such as combat pilots. For it would enable them to avoid hazards during 'low' periods or, if that were impossible, to exercise special care and vigilance.

L-field measurements can also be useful in agriculture. By measuring the L-fields of seeds it is possible to predict how strong and healthy the future plant will be.[20] And in measuring the L-fields of plants it has been found that the change of a single gene in the parent stock produces changes in the voltage pattern.[21] This discovery could be of importance to the study of genetics in plants and animals.

It is probable that the reader is no more interested in breeding frogs than the writer. But one of Dr. Burr's earliest discoveries should be mentioned because it is most significant: measurement of the voltages in different parts of the field of a frog's egg can show the *future* location of the frog's nervous system.[22]

This is important because it shows that the L-field is the controlling, organizing force in the growth of the living form —an electrical 'matrix' which moulds living matter. It is also another illustration of the important fact that the field *anticipates* physical conditions.

We have already seen other examples of this: a voltage-rise in the field *anticipates* ovulation; abnormal voltage-patterns *anticipate* the physical symptoms of malignancy and the emotional symptoms of mental instability; and the state of the field in a seed shows how strong and healthy the *future* plant will be. All this shows that the field is master, so to speak, and that matter is its slave.

Another significant property of L-fields is that they are integrated, overriding *units*. This is shown by the fact that such conditions as ovulation or malignancy can be detected by measuring the field of the human body *at a distance from the affected organs*. The striking voltage-rise, for instance, that precedes ovulation can be measured merely by dipping the fingers into dishes of solution connected to a voltmeter— which is how Dr. Burr's married patient measured her own L-field and learned that ovulation was imminent.

It has also been found that it is sometimes possible to measure field voltages with the electrodes a millimetre or more *away from the surface of the skin—not* in contact with it. This proves that it is a true field which is being measured and not some surface electrical potentials.

All this shows that the L-field for any given living form is an integral, controlling unit and that the sub-fields of the various organs, cells, molecules and atoms within the form must be subordinate to the overall L-field.

6

Though there is no mystery about measuring L-fields some experience and technical 'know-how' are required. And for the reader who is not interested in technicalities it is probably sufficient to know that the highly-sensitive voltmeters used are now commercially-available and are standard equipment in many electronic laboratories. As they are expensive to buy and tricky to use in measuring L-fields, the non-technical reader need not feel that he ought to get one for his bathroom; and can cheerfully skip to Section 7 of this chapter.

Scientifically-inclined readers, however, may like to have some technical details:

As stated above, the voltage-gradients in L-fields are pure direct-current *potentials,* quite different from the electrical impulses measured in the brain or the heart. To measure potential differences between different parts of the L-field, it is necessary to use an instrument which draws virtually no current and therefore does not drain away the potential. For this purpose the vacuum-tube voltmeter is the most convenient and reliable.

Today various kinds of standard vacuum-tube voltmeter can be used. But in the days when Dr. Burr started his research these were not available and he had to develop his own, with the help of Dr. Cecil Lane, of the Department of Physics, Yale University. Together they built a balanced bridge vacuum-tube voltmeter with an input impedance of ten million ohms, which was considered high in those days.

This was not so easy as it may seem to the modern electronics engineer. By modern standards tubes were crude and the choice limited. They had to find the right tubes to use and to balance one tube against the other so that changes in the electron input to one tube could be balanced against the input to a second tube linked to ground. As tubes were not made so uniformly as they are today, they had to match one tube against another.[23]

With the improvement of tubes and with the development of the whole electronic science this tedious work is no longer necessary; and the best instrument-makers can supply suitable voltmeters ready-made. A suitable American type is the H.P. Precision Volt-ohm-ammeter, Model No. H.P 412 A, made by the Hewlett-Packard Company, of Palo Alto, California. No doubt there are suitable British or European equivalents. It is essential that the input resistance of any voltmeter used should exceed ten megohms; and the instrument should be provided with a plus and minus scale, with zero at the centre.

Proper electrodes are vital. Dr. Burr used silver-silverchloride electrodes, which are non-polarizable and reversible and which remain constant for long periods of time—some were used in the tree-potential measurements for over thirty years. These electrodes are made in matched pairs of the size most appropriate for the L-field that is to be measured. They are prepared by immersing clean and pure silver wire or plate in *molten* silver-chloride of high purity.

These electrodes are never in actual contact with the surface of the skin, organ or specimen. They are separated from the surface by a 'bridge' of physiological salt-solution or paste, of approximately the same ionic concentration as the fluids of living organisms. They are matched so that there is little or no self-potential of the electrodes.

Physiological salt solutions are convenient for some measurements—for instance, when the index fingers are dipped into little dishes of solution in which the electrodes are immersed. They were used in what scientists would describe as one of Dr. Burr's most 'elegant' experiments: to demonstrate the L-field of a salamander.

He floated the salamander in a circular dish of solution which was slowly rotated. Because salamanders, like every living thing, have a field, the rotating animal behaved exactly like the armature of a dynamo and generated an alternating electrical output which was displayed on a recording galvanometer as a perfect sine wave.[24]

For most measurements it is more convenient to use a neutral paste—such as Park Davis 'Unibase'—to which has been added nine-tenths of 1 per cent sodium chloride. This paste prevents direct contact between the silver-chloride of the electrode and the surface of the living organism and eliminates possible errors from any potential of the electrode.

To measure tree-potentials Dr. Burr used small plastic containers full of paste with one surface open. The electrodes were embedded in the paste and the open surface of the paste-filled container held against the cambium layer of the tree. The other electrode was similarly applied at a vertical distance from the other of two or three feet.

To measure the fields of very small organisms, such as seeds or frog's eggs, it is necessary to use micro-pipettes filled with physiological salt solution, with the electrodes in the upper ends. Obviously this calls for great technical skill.

To measure the state of the whole human L-field, one electrode is normally attached to the forehead and the other one either to the chest or to the palm of one hand, both of course separated from the surface of the skin with a 'bridge' of the paste described above. Or the field can be measured, as already mentioned, by dipping the index finger of each hand into dishes of salt solution in which the electrodes are immersed. The fingers are then reversed to get an average reading.

If it is desired to measure the electrical condition of some specific part of the body—say, the cervix—one electrode immersed in paste is held in contact with, or close to, the cervix and the other applied to some convenient point of reference, such as the ankle.

Careful grounding or earthing of various parts of the equipment and circuitry is imperative; and special precautions must be taken because there is often a potential difference between two grounding-rods driven into the earth as close as three feet apart.

Electrical, radio and telephone engineers assume that any area of ground has the same zero potential all over; and for their practical purposes it has. But in measuring L-fields, it

37

must be remembered that there is no such thing as a 'common ground'; and all ground connections must be made to the same rod driven into the ground.

When Dr. Burr was measuring tree-potentials in relation to telluric currents he made the disconcerting discovery that there were fluctuating potential differences between two monel-metal rods driven into the ground only a yard apart. So it will be obvious that, if one part of the equipment is grounded at a point separated from the ground of another part, telluric potentials could introduce errors.

Provided good equipment is properly installed and suitable precautions taken it is not hard to measure the voltage-gradients in the human L-field because these are usually of the order of millivolts, even in the case of mental effects. *Dr. Ravitz has found, for instance, that even a strong emotion recalled under hypnosis can cause a voltage change of between 15 and 20 millivolts.*

To interpret the voltage-gradients demands, of course, some experience and some medical or psychiatric knowledge. But the writer has been assured that any good technician can soon be taught to measure voltage-gradients and that any intelligent person can be taught to interpret the voltage readings after a short period of intensive instruction. As the readings are purely quantitative they are easier to interpret than X-ray photographs.

Doctors of the future are unlikely to own and use electrometric equipment themselves because its proper operation demands time and some specialized knowledge. It is probable that they will send their patients to medical laboratories to have their L-fields measured and interpreted in much the same way as they send them to radiologists today.

Meanwhile it should be obvious that the discovery of L-fields opens up an enormous field for creative medical and biological research. It is wide open for exploration by anyone who is willing to buy the equipment, to study the numerous scientific papers by Dr. Burr and his associates and to learn the techniques by experience. And the next time a Foundation with more money than purpose finds an Income Tax Inspector breathing down its neck or some government research organization is asked awkward questions by the politicians it could not do anything more useful than to promote further research into L-fields by some imaginative and open-minded scientists. For L-fields are the basis of all life on this planet.

There are other opportunities for research apart from those indicated above because it may prove possible to treat various physical ills by direct electrical treatment of the controlling L-field. Though not enough research has been done to be certain about this, there is some evidence that it is quite likely:

Alternating electromagnetic fields of certain highly-specific frequencies applied to the L-field of the body seem to reduce blood-pressure and cholesterol-levels. It has been reported that the healing of wounds in experimental animals can be speeded up by subjecting them to an electrical field. And the writer has seen a report from Germany which claims beneficial effects on human patients by placing them in an intense electrostatic field.

Much work will have to be done before we can know whether electrical treatment of L-fields will prove to be a useful tool of medicine. But the possibility is worth mentioning.

7

How does all this affect the claims made for genes and DNA?

Though genes and molecules are too small for their electro-magnetic fields to be measured directly, they are ultimately composed—like all matter—of atoms, which are known to contain fields. It is safe to assume, therefore, that genes, like all living forms possess their characteristic little L-fields and that the DNA molecule also has a field. But all these are within the overall L-field of the body and though, no doubt, there is 'feed-back'—that is, they have some influence on the overall field—they must be subject to its overriding control and must therefore be considered sub-ordinate factors in our make-up, even though their influence may be important. Probably, they are some of the 'tools' used by the L-field.

There are other reasons for supposing that they are sub-ordinate:

1. A part cannot be a matrix for a whole; a simple design cannot be a blue-print for a more complicated one. As a functioning organization, the body is more than the sum of its components. Genes and DNA molecules are simpler organizations than the organization of the body *as a whole*.

2. As we have seen, the L-field can anticipate or predict. It can anticipate ovulation, predict in which part of a frog's egg the nervous system will develop and how strong and healthy a future plant will be.

Though it may well have happened, this reporter has not yet heard that biochemists endow their pet molecules with powers of prediction or regard DNA as a molecular Jeane Dixon. But the L-field has to know the body's needs *in advance*—especially during growth—and to arrange to send supplies or replacements *to the right place at the right time*— a problem in logistics which would tax the talents of an experienced Quartermaster and which seems a little beyond the powers of a mere molecule.

3. It is true that DNA-fans credit molecules with anthropomorphic powers, in much the same way as primitive tribes attribute human attributes to idols of stone or wood. They solemnly assure us that Molecule A has all the information needed for heredity, that Molecule B passes this on to the cells while Molecule C assesses the needs of the cells and restrains A and B from getting too enthusiastic. But nobody has so far explained *how* Molecule A got the information in the first place, *how* Molecule B distributes it and *how* Molecule C can judge anything, let alone check A and B.

All this unproven supposition—perhaps superstition would be more accurate—quite overlooks not only the *proven* existence of the overriding L-field but also other things which we shall consider later.

4. It seems to be supposed that DNA and genes act as matrices which enables molecules and cells to 'replicate' themselves. This ignores the fact that a matrix, to be any use at all, must be quite independent of—and unaffected by— the stuff that it moulds. If, for instance, a mould dissolved in the molten metal of a casting it would be useless as a mould. Since the molecules of the body are constantly breaking down or reacting with each other, they cannot serve as matrices

themselves. They may serve, however, to localize or 'anchor' little fields which serve as matrices.

5. A matrix which can maintain a constant pattern of ever-changing material must itself be relatively permanent. Since the cells and molecules of the body are always being torn apart and re-built, whatever keeps them in constant pattern must not change. Therefore it cannot be chemical and must be of a different nature.

6. Atomic fission has shown that matter—once considered 'solid'—can sometimes be converted into waves of energy. Nuclear physics has shown that atoms—of which every material thing is built—are composed largely of space, filled with fields and particles in motion—particles which sometimes behave more like waves than particles.

Field physics recognizes that there are many fields in nature —with their associated particles—which interact with one another. These range from tiny fields within the atom to vast gravitational and other fields of stars and planets which can exert their influence across great distances. The moon, for instance, produces tides within the field of the earth.

Is there any reason to suppose that the human body is a miraculous exception to the universal rule of fields and is organized by some mystical, unexplained chemistry? Surely it is more reasonable to suppose that genes and DNA produce their effects by means of their inherent fields? For fields cannot be affected by chemical changes and can, in fact, control them.

7. If we agree on this, we must also accept that the influence of the fields of genes and DNA is subordinate to that of the greater L-field, of which they are a part.

In their present preoccupation with particles, biology and biochemistry are in the same stage that physics was years ago before 'particle physics' gave place to 'field physics'. When, one day, biology matures and 'particle biology' gives way to 'field biology' the role of genes and DNA will be seen in true perspective.

CHAPTER THREE

First Clues

'Their science roamed from star to star
And than itself found nothing greater.
What wonder? In a Leyden Jar
They bottled the creator.'[1]

1

What has the discovery of L-fields got to do with our four questions? Quite a lot.

First of all it shows that there is much more to man—even physically—than mere chemistry. He is not the illegitimate offspring of accidental atomic intercourse nor the end-product of some cosmic chowder of proteins, cooked by lightning when the earth was young, as some would have us believe. He depends for his growth, maintenance and existence on an invisible, intangible, *organizing* field.

For anything that organizes is, of course, the opposite of chance. So the discovery of L-fields contradicts theories of 'blind chance' and also devalues modern ideas of genes bounding about *at random*. Since the discovery of L-fields, then, such notions as 'we are what our genes make us' or 'love is only chemistry' look even sillier than many already thought.

Not long after Dr. Burr and Dr. Northrop discovered L-fields, by the way, another deadly blow to 'blind chance' theories was administered by Dr. Pierre Lecomte de Noüy. As the latter demonstrated, in his famous book, *Human Destiny*[2] the mathematical probabilities against even one protein molecule being created by sheer chance, still less a complete living form, are so overwhelming as to be inconceivable.

Second, our bodies, then, are the product of organization: and, in all our experience, *organization of any kind involves both foresight and purpose*. So the fact that man is controlled by an organizing field implies that human existence has purpose.

Third, though the human L-field, with all its sub-fields, is unimaginably complicated—it *has* to be to control so complex an organization as the human body—it is still an electromagnetic field, with the properties of the simpler fields known to physics. Like them, then, it is included in the more powerful fields of the Universe and subject to their influence. (It was mentioned in the previous chapter that the L-fields of trees are affected by both lunar cycles and sun-spots and, although it is not yet known if human L-fields are similarly affected, it is highly probable. Evidence of this is that maternity hospitals often have to handle more births per day than usual during the period of the full moon.)

Since the human L-field is included in—and subject to—the more powerful fields of the Universe, man is an integral part of the organization of the Universe, *subject to all its laws and a participant in its purpose*. He may be one of Nature's more ambitious experiments—at least in this neck of the Milky Way—but, with all the millions of stars and, probably, planets to use as laboratories it seems probable that Nature has lots of bigger and better experiments going on elsewhere. To suppose otherwise would be to take a dim view of Nature's ingenuity and enterprise. In any case, it is evident that man is not a special creation outside and apart from all the rest, nor a mysterious exception to the general rule.

If all this conflicts with the cherished notions of some scientists,* it is in harmony with the trend of modern physics, which is based on the brilliant thinking of such geniuses as James Clerk Maxwell or Albert Einstein. The mathematical laws which they discovered are exact expressions of perfect organization.

Towards the end of his life, too, as everyone knows, Einstein was trying to work out a 'unified field theory' to embrace all the fields of the Universe; and for years he had

---

* A distinguished exception is Professor Edwin Conklin, the great Princeton biologist, who is reported to have said: 'The probability of life originating from accident is comparable to the probability of the Unabridged Dictionary resulting from an explosion in a printing factory.'

been trying to reject the concept of matter and to build a pure field physics. He is also said to have remarked that 'God does not play dice.' This shows that he realized that fields are the regulators of everything that exists and that the Universe is the product of organization, not chance.

If it were not, it is doubtful whether it could ever have continued to exist for more than a few seconds. With everything, from stars to atoms, in constant motion, unless there were organization and regulators, such as fields, chaos would be instantaneous and complete.

Even if an unorganized Universe were possible and somehow managed to teeter along, there could be no science. With no natural laws to discover, with no predictable phenomena to study and develop, all our scientists would be as unemployable as carpenters without lumber or plumbers without pipes. Yet one of the diverting spectacles of these times are some lesser lights of science who affect to believe in blind chance without realizing that science depends on exactly the opposite.

Somewhere in the middle, most professional philosophers admit that the Universe is organized but seem to shy away from committing themselves to any kind of 'organizer', partly perhaps, because they have no idea what it could be like and partly, perhaps, because they fear that to admit the existence of an organizer might also imply an admission of religious or mystical factors. They could overcome both these problems by studying fields, which are not in the least religious and not too mystical to be measured with a voltmeter.

2

As electromagnetic fields, L-fields have properties which suggest, at least, some interesting possibilities.

Fields are very stable things. They can travel through space and preserve their identity over vast distances and for immense periods of time. And the only way to destroy a field is to remove its source. As we do not know the source of L-fields we can say that we, at least, know no way to destroy them.

Anything that can organize has to exist *before* whatever it organizes—no organization can start without a previous plan.

If it is argued that lots of organizations do, particularly in Washington, D.C., the answer is that there is always some kind of plan, even if it is only to promote Parkinson's Law and to create more jobs.

Human L-fields, then, must exist before they start the job of organizing the embryo in the womb; frog L-fields must exist before the egg starts to develop and, as proof of this, we have seen that they can show along which axis of the egg the future frog's nervous system will develop.

There is no reason to suppose, too, that L-fields cease to exist when the bodies they have organized die and decompose, any more than a magnet's field ceases to exist when the iron filings it has formed into a pattern are thrown away. The body is not the source of the field, merely its result and unless the source is removed the field must continue to exist—ready, no doubt, to organize future bodies when opportunity offers.

Professor G. D. Wasserman, the British mathematician, has suggested the probable explanation[3] that what we have called L-fields—and what he calls M- (morphogenetic) fields—exist in 'latent' form in space ready to enter into a 'bound state' with specific organizations of matter such as an ovum. But, he suggests, they cannot do this and start to organize the future form until a sperm has changed the 'quantum state' of the ovum in such a way that the 'steering' field can commence to organize the future form.

M. Jean Rostand, a leading French biologist, has stated that man has long since ceased to evolve and that modern man does not differ essentially from human beings who lived 100,000 years ago.[4] This indicates that Nature has long been satisfied with the general design of the human body, sees no point in changing her 'blue-prints' and uses the same old L-fields over and over again.

All this suggests an answer to our question: 'Where do we come from?' as far as *our bodies only* are concerned. We can think of this planet as being saturated with innumerable L-fields for all the different forms of life that can exist on it. When an ovum is fertilized or a plant pollinated there is an opportunity for an appropriate L-field to start organizing a body or a plant around a nucleus of matter.

We should remember that electromagnetic fields can vary in size from the tiny to the enormous and can travel through space at the speed of light. There is no problem, therefore, about an L-field 'finding' a suitable nucleus and taking it over almost instantaneously after fertilization.

Since conception is merely the fusion of two *already-existing* tiny organizations, the sperm and the ovum, it *creates nothing, except an opportunity* and the right conditions for an L-field to start its work. When the ovum has been fertilized, the appropriate L-field is attracted—borrowed, if you will—from the always available 'pool' of 'latent' fields.

This L-field immediately starts to organize the future form around the nucleus of the ovum by a process of organized cell-division. For this it needs materials, which it borrows, through the food supplied by the mother, from the reservoir of materials available on this planet. This process of borrowing materials, *via* the food, and returning them to the earth and atmosphere as waste products goes on throughout the life of the form until, when the body dies—the L-field is released to return to the common pool and all the borrowed materials are returned to the reservoirs of matter—'earth to earth, dust to dust'—subject to some delays due to modern undertaking practices.

An analogy may help to clarify the picture. This planet is currently—and unfortunately—saturated with countless electromagnetic fields set up by thousands of radio, television and radar transmitters. These are passing around and through us all the time, but luckily, we are not conscious of these fields because they cannot manifest as sound—or pictures on a tube—unless we provide the right equipment and tune it properly.

Similarly, the ubiquitous L-fields cannot manifest as living forms until they find the right, 'pre-tuned' equipment—a fertilized ovum or fertile seed.

This picture of L-fields from a common pool being used over and over can explain not only why modern man is not too different from humans who lived 100,000 years ago but also why all human bodies today have the same general design. Alert readers of the *National Geographic Magazine* will have noticed that the bodies of the most primitive tribes do not differ essentially from what they see in their own bathroom mirrors.

It should be emphasized that all this refers to *our physical bodies only*. We shall consider the problem of mind and personality later.

3

If Barbara Tuchman is right about the disastrous effects of the Theory of Evolution—see page 1—perhaps we should examine it in the light of L-fields before we go any further.

It is, of course, *only* a theory which has never been proved, even though the strident claims of geneticists sometimes give that impression. But more and more irreverent thinkers are beginning to question the Darwinian Encyclicals.

In a book,[5] published as long ago as 1958, the late Professor H. Graham Cannon, F.R.S., the eminent British zoologist, challenged the dogma that blind chance is the mainspring of evolution. He also maintained that the gene theory cannot possibly account for the capacity of an organism not only to admit new characters but also to adjust the functioning of its existing parts so that the organism forms a new whole and works as a new unit.

Professor Cannon's studies of experimental embryology convinced him that the wonderfully-precise and efficient mechanisms of living things could not have been brought about by pure chance. He wrote:

'. . . as an evolutionary mechanism Mendelism can only be successful in relation to trivial characters, to characters of no selective value. . . . Mendelism can only be concerned with . . . the twigs of the evolutionary tree. . . .

'. . . evolution, that gradual unfolding, is dependent on something else than the playthings of the Neo-Mendelians. It has taken place, not by virtue of a succession of lucky chances but as the result of something central, which is inherent in all living things—an expression of inexorable physico-chemical law . . . this law of evolution is something of sheer beauty because of its omnipotence and what Power there must be behind it is something very wonderful. . . .

47

'Always this Power, this organismal control, is there to see that the organism is in the right state at the right time. . . .'

If L-fields do not represent the whole 'organismal control' to which Professor Cannon refers, clearly they are an important part of it.

Ten years before Professor Cannon's book was published, a distinguished astronomer, Dr. Gustaf Strömberg, pointed out some holes in the leaky hull of the Theory, which the evolutionists have not been able to plug: [6]

'It is significant that *new forms of life have appeared on earth rather suddenly*, and that both ancient and modern organic life is represented by *standard types and species* of organisms, instead of by a more uniform sequence of living forms as might be expected if the change had been more gradual.

'It is no wonder that *some authorities in biology are now convinced that mutations are insufficient to explain the origin of life and the more radical changes in evolution*. . . .

'As the matter in the earth is part of the original matter of the Universe, so life on earth is part of the original life of the Universe.' (Our italics.)

L-fields can plug these holes—if they are worth plugging—because, as electromagnetic fields, they can exist apart from matter and travel through space. They could account, therefore, for the fact that 'new forms of life have appeared on earth rather suddenly', as Dr. Strömberg says. And they can account for the 'origin of life' and also the 'more radical changes in evolution'.

On the other hand, the discovery of L-fields rips a gash in the hull of the Theory of *Titanic* proportions because L-fields organize and control living forms but are themselves non-material. For this reason they cannot possibly be the *result* of *physical evolution*, even though they may sometimes be modified by 'feed-back' from the matter that they organize. And, as organizers, they can have nothing to do with chance.

Since L-fields, too, are non-material it is not necessary to

assume that they must have been designed or developed in
association with the matter of this planet, any more than an
architect's plans have to be drawn on the site. L-fields might
well have been designed elsewhere—in Nature's 'drawing-
office', so to speak—and sent to this planet to take material
form.

Whether or not they were designed 'on the site', the fact
that L-fields can exist apart from the matter they organize
solves a problem which evolutionists prefer to ignore. This
is that the development of living forms on this planet has
probably been interrupted by cataclysms and vast climatic
changes which would have made the 'slow, orderly process of
evolution' of the Theory difficult if not impossible.

Even if Dr. Velikovsky is mistaken in suggesting that cataclysms wiped out most of the life on earth in relatively-recent
times, there is plenty of evidence in different parts of the
world that the earth has undergone climatic changes, drastic
enough to interfere with the 'slow, orderly process'. Coal from
decayed tropical vegetation, for instance, is now found in cold
regions while mammoths were mysteriously trapped by an
instant freeze in Siberia.

Though cataclysms or climatic changes could destroy a lot
of living forms or even all of them—human, animals or
plants—they would have no effect whatever on L-fields. These
could continue to saturate this planet for any length of time
until conditions for organizing new life became favourable
again. Previous to that, of course, the fields of such components of living forms as DNA and protein molecules would
have produced these when conditions allowed, if they had not
survived the cataclysms.

Since human L-fields cannot be the product of physical
evolution, it is not necessary to assume that the human body
has evolved from lower forms of life. Nature is so ingenious
and so lavish with her designs and produces such an infinite
variety that it would be no problem for her to produce the
L-fields for humans, apes and other forms of life, quite independently of each other.

It is true that she finds it convenient to use components
or 'sub-assemblies'—such as lungs, livers, hearts, hormones
and so on—which are similar or identical in design in many

species. And the overall design of apes is very similar to that of humans. But it does not necessarily follow that she had to try out all these sub-assemblies in lower forms of life before she could use them in higher ones. For all we know, she could easily have designed components which could be used in many different species and also designed the species themselves, all at the same time.

We have seen that L-fields have to anticipate. In organizing the growth of a human embryo, for instance, they have to know where specialized cells will be needed and to plan their arrangement in advance. As Professor Cannon put it: 'Always this . . . organismal control is there to see that the organism is in the right state at the right time.' Obviously, Nature, the designer of L-fields, can anticipate infinitely better and on a cosmic scale because the organization of the Universe would have been quite impossible without forethought.

There is evidence all around us that Nature is no fumbling hobbyist. To suggest, then, that she has to feel her way by trial and error is to compare the Designer of the Universe to the Market Research Division of some advertising agency, which has to try out a new Instant Shampoo on the ladies of Moline, Ill., for 'customer acceptance assessments' before it can be sure whether the new product will be viable in the market.

That is not to suggest that Nature always produces all her designs full-blown but merely that she *need* not do so if she does not want to. She may evolve many of them from simpler forms for interest—or amusement—and it certainly seems that the whole trend of her experiments is towards increasing complexity. But this does not mean that our bodies necessarily evolved from lower forms of life.

A good reason for thinking that they did not is that there is a wide and unbridged gap between animals and humans and, so far, nobody has found a satisfactory 'missing link'. One skull in which evolutionists placed touching faith for many years turned out to be a brillant practical joke.

It is true that some men, of the all-in wrestler type, are faintly reminiscent of gorillas. But any resemblance between, say, a nude in *Playboy* magazine and a female ape is purely incidental; pictures of the latter stir no human male pulses.

It has to be admitted, too, that the character of some humans, notably in the totalitarian states, seems to be on the same level as that of orangutans—and sometimes much lower. But there is still a wide difference in other qualities: no ape or orangutan has ever qualified for human occupations even in a dictator's Secret Police.

One might reasonably expect the 'slow, orderly process' of evolution from lower forms—and billions of genes rattling about for thousands of years, selecting themselves 'naturally' —to have done better than this. Surely these processes should, by now, have been able to produce a few semi-anthropoid candidates for a 'Miss Africa' jungle-beauty contest or a few half-apes qualified at least to be nightclub bouncers or Mafia executioners?

But the great gap between man and animal has neither been bridged nor explained and hopes of finding a 'missing link' are growing fainter.

Not many years ago, in fact, things were made even more difficult by the discovery of the bones of 'long-jawed, dog-toothed primates' in East Africa by Professor Wilfred Le Gros Clark, of Oxford. To some experts these seemed more likely —and, perhaps, more attractive—ancestors of man than apes. But in reporting this discovery, a correspondent of the *New York Times* observed: [7]

'At the moment the possible discovery of anything like a missing link seems even less likely than the ascent of man from the gibbon and gorilla.'

With the enthusiasm of hungry terriers, hundreds of men for a hundred years have been feverishly grubbing up old bones in many parts of the world but, at this writing, have never found anything that could pass for a link between man and ape or even between man and 'long-jawed, dog-toothed primates'. This suggests that Nature made a 'custom' design for human L-fields but—with her usual efficiency and economy—incorporated standard components which she also used in lower forms of life. For, without being too pleased with ourselves we can claim that Nature planned a rather higher destiny for man than for apes and may well have thought that man needed a custom-designed body. And she could easily have produced that design somewhere else and sent it to earth for production.

It is perhaps worth noting that certain ancient legends tell us that something like this happened; and ancient legends, however 'far out' they may seem, sometimes have a basis of truth.*

4

Whether our bodies have or have not evolved from animal forms is actually unimportant *in itself*, as we shall see. But, when the Theory of Evolution is used to justify such things as German militarism, we cannot afford to ignore it any more than we can afford to ignore the theories of Karl Marx, which had equally unfortunate consequences. For, militarism apart, the Theory has needlessly deprived uncounted people of any sustaining faith, of any sense of purpose, of any hope and, sometimes, of any sense of responsibility.

When, for example, the Darwin disciples met in Chicago to celebrate the centennial of the Master's Theory, Sir Julian Huxley expounded what, presumably, is the official creed of the evolutionists—as reported by the Associated Press.[8]

'In the evolutionary pattern of thought, there is no longer either need or room for supernatural beings capable of affecting the course of events.

'The earth was not created, it evolved. So did all the animals and plants that inhabit it, including our human selves,

---

* For example, there is an intriguing and mysterious reference in the Book of Genesis 6:1: 'And it came to pass, when men began to multiply on the face of the earth and daughters were born unto them, that the sons of God saw the daughters of men that they were fair; and they took them wives of all which they chose. . . .

'There were giants in the earth in those days; and also after that, when the sons of God came in unto the daughters of men, and they bare children to them, the same became mighty men which were of old, men of renown.'

This suggests that 'Adam and Eve' and their immediate descendants may have had inferior or even ape-like forms which were upgraded to human form by the introduction of superior L-fields from elsewhere; and that this produced a superior breed which—by comparison with the original ape-like inhabitants of earth—seemed like 'giants' and 'mighty men.'

mind and soul, as well as brain and body.

'So did religion. They (religions) are organizations of human thought. . . . In this they resembled other early organizations of human thought confronted with nature, like the doctrine of the four elements—earth, air, fire and water. . . .

'Like these they are destined to disappear in competition with other truer and more embracing thought organizations which are handling the same range of raw or processed experience.'

Since this gem of eloquence was addressed to the converted, probably nobody thought to ask the distinguished speaker where earth got the raw material to evolve with or how physical evolution can possibly create 'organizations of thought' which are non-physical. And nobody seemed to find it amusing that this apostle of the doctrine of natural selection —a chancy process—should have to use the word 'organization'—the antithesis of chance—no less than three times in two paragraphs.

But perhaps his fascinated listeners were content to await a further thrilling instalment of the evolutionary dogma after 'truer and more embracing thought organizations' have finished 'handling the same range of raw or processed experience'—whatever that may mean.

No doubt Sir Julian honestly believed what he said and, of course, had a perfect right to say it. But such remarks, coming from so well-known a scientist, are likely to discourage a lot of people who take all scientists as seriously as Africans used to take their witch-doctors. For there are millions who are desperately searching for some hope and purpose in life and who would like to believe that their religions are something more than 'organizations of human thought' which are 'destined to disappear'.

Many of them may not realize that scientists who deny the existence of organization in the Universe, scientists who try to 'bottle the creator'—as the verse at the head of this chapter puts it—are probably only a small vociferous minority and do not represent the point of view of most scientists. The latter may not all be religious but are compelled by their observations, if not by their emotions, to realize that there is some organizing agency behind all natural phenomena and the Universe itself.

As human developments go, modern science, despite its great achievements, is still in early adolescence. Many of its practitioners, in fact, are rather like 'overgrown schoolboys who like to take things apart', as a great scientist once explained to the writer. And a certain amount of arrogance is normal among adolescents, as any parent knows.

This problem is realized by some of the wisest scientists themselves. As Dr. Ralph Wyckoff, the distinguished physicist and crystallographer, has so aptly put it: [9]

'Those of us who have growing children know how inevitably the period of passive and dependent childhood is followed by an aggressively assertive adolescence. . . . We are now in the adolescence of the human intellect, with all its attendant dangers and all its magnificent promise for a more adult future.

'It is this immature arrogance of the intellect that was so largely responsible for the grossly materialistic phase of human thought from which there are signs that we are emerging; *but there are still plenty of intellectuals who are sure that their present vision encompasses the knowable.*' (Our italics.)

It is unfortunate that the present vision of the evolutionists does not seem to encompass a knowledge of the electromagnetic fields of life, even though these have been known for thirty years.

Or perhaps they prefer to ignore them, hoping that if they do so they will go away. This would be understandable because the existence of organizing L-fields has been proved by experiment and anyone can measure them. But theories of blind chance and natural selection have never been proved and nothing about them can be measured—not even the perfervid enthusiasm of their apostles.

CHAPTER FOUR

Glimpses of the Obvious

'THINK'
—*I.B.M.*

1

In the distant days when this reporter had reasons to visit the World Headquarters of the International Business Machines Corporation, a wall-placard—'THINK'—in large letters was mandatory—perhaps still is—in the office of every executive. And wags who dared to add: 'OR THWIM' were viewed with disfavour by Top Management.

Though executives of less successful corporations thought this requirement funny, the fabulous success of I.B.M. is sufficient evidence that thinking can be a solid asset to business. This, in fact, is usually conceded in theory by most business executives. But, in practice, they are usually so busy telephoning, dictating or attending conferences that the tedious chore of thinking has to be left to droves of attorneys, business consultants or assorted college graduates hired for the purpose.

In business circles, too, thinking does not really count as work and it is important for the ambitious executive always to give the impression of being busy and on the go. So he would far sooner be caught stark naked in the office than sitting in his chair merely thinking as this would give the impression of not being sufficiently 'aggressive'.

Lip-service, at least, is paid to thinking by the educational industry. Some of the more progressive establishments, in fact, even attempt to encourage it in any odd moments that can be spared from injecting sufficient memorized information into students to enable them to hoard the academic coinage of 'credits'.

Scientists are more or less forced to think in order to 'publish or perish'; and most of them have a hard time fitting in thinking between looking for research grants, force-feeding students with facts and attending the essential professional wingdings.

It may safely be said, then, that this civilization regards thinking as a respectable and even, sometimes, necessary way of spending time. But, strangely enough, *thinking about thinking*—trying to find out what thinking and thought are —is considered a slightly lunatic, not-quite-respectable, and almost Un-American activity.*

There are several reasons for this. Perhaps the chief one is that thought and thinking cannot be measured and experiments with thought are often not 'repeatable' for reasons we shall see shortly. Thinking and thought, therefore, are automatically 'unscientific' and beneath the notice of science, even though scientists themselves have to think, if it is only to write a paper, drive the car or fry an egg.

Then the biologists and biochemists like to claim that thinking is a purely physico-chemical process, though they entirely fail to explain it. But, like little dogs with a bone too big for them to handle, they keep worrying it and doing everything possible to scare off others who might know what to do with it.

For these reasons, research into thought is not encouraged by the Scientific Establishment and those who indulge in it are often ridiculed and sometimes ostracized. So some useful clues to what thought is have been lying around unnoticed for a long time.

On the other hand, men and women can—and often do— think much more, apparently, than the lower animals. So we cannot hope properly to answer our four questions unless we are ready to examine this aspect of man, even at the risk of being thought queer, unscientific and even Un-American.

* Since this was written the Parapsycholocal Association of the United States has been admitted as an affiliate of the American Association for the Advancement of Science, over the objections of some members who still feel that parapsychological research is not true science.

2

Those who would have us believe that thinking is a purely physico-chemical process overlook one important fact: while our memory of knowledge acquired, on which our thinking is based, is permanent, the matter of the brain, like that of our bodies, is constantly changing, as we saw in Chapter 2. To quote Sir Charles Sherrington again:[1] 'The brain is, of course . . . composed like other body organs of just physico-chemical stuff, which breaks down finally into waste products.'

Another authority, Dr. R. W. Gerard, Irving Professor of Biology and Dean Emeritus, University of California, has written:[2]

'It is now a truism that metabolism is necessary to function: that cells, tissues, organisms are dynamic machines and must pay for what they do. . . .
'Quantitatively the metabolism of the nervous system is high. Peripheral nerve and muscle have about the same rate of respiration, nerve not being lower as many believe; and the central nervous system, whether in the frog or the mammal, enjoys an oxygen consumption some 30 times greater than does the peripheral nerve. . . . It is not surprising, for example, that . . . *the brain, though constituting only 2% of the body weight of man, contributes 10% of the basal metabolism.*' (Our italics.)

Some years ago, Dr. Paul Weiss, of the Rockefeller Institution, reported to the National Academy of Sciences that the nervous system, including the brain cells, is being constantly regenerated.

His experiments 'prove that the elements of the nervous system are by no means static and immutable fixtures . . . but are in a dynamic state of constant self-renewal. . . . This introduces a new dimension into our concepts of adaptive and operative mechanisms of nervous and mental functions, including learning.'[3]

Webster defines metabolism as 'the sum of the processes concerned in the building up of protoplasm and its destruction incidental to life; the chemical changes in living cells, by which the energy is provided for the vital processes and activities and new material is assimilated to repair the waste'. And Dr. Gerard reports that the brain accounts for 10% of the basal metabolism of the body.

With the materials of the brain breaking down and being renewed even faster than some other parts of the body, how can this changing chemistry hold or use the knowledge we need for thinking, let alone do any thinking on its own?

A simple example will show how improbable this is: when, say, we make up our personal accounts we use the knowledge of how to add and subtract which we acquired in childhood and which has been fixed in our memories ever since Yet the material of our brain-cells and of their connecting nerves may have been completely renewed as many as a hundred times since we were taught addition and subtraction.

Does not this suggest that we must possess something more stable and permanent than the seething chemistry of the brain to keep our memories in shape?

Since our bodies have to have an electromagnetic field to organize and maintain them, surely our thoughts and memories must need something similar even more?

That, of course, is exactly what they do have and the evidence for it is one of those things so absurdly obvious that they are often overlooked.

When a thought is transmitted from the mind of one person to the mind of another—an everyday phenomenon—something occurs at one point in space because something else happened at another point, with no visible means by which the 'cause' can be related to the 'effect'. When this happens —it will be remembered—physicists say that the two events are connected by a 'field'.

So the phenomenon of thought-transmission shows that *thought has the properties of a field*—within the accepted definition of a field.

We shall find that this simple, obvious fact offers us the clue to many problems. But, first, we must deal with the inevitable objection that 'science has proved that there is no such thing as thought-transmission'.

Though this is a common superstition, the fact is that science has proved nothing of the sort, because to ignore or to ridicule something is not to disprove it. Science, as a whole, has made no serious study of thought-transmission but that—as noted above—has not prevented science ridiculing and even ostracizing those who have.

Without benefit of science, thought-transmission has been an *experimentally-proven fact* to countless people since the beginning of man's history. It is an accepted commonplace among husbands and wives, parents and children and others who are mutually-sympathetic. Primitive but perceptive peoples—though officially 'underdeveloped'—have been using thought-transmission for centuries. And the literature of the subject—far too voluminous to be quoted here—offers more well-attested proof of thought-transmission than most scientists can muster to support their pet theories.

Many readers, no doubt, will have had personal experience of it. If not, it is probable that they have trusted friends who can give them proof.

On at least two occasions, mind reading—a form of thought-transmission—has actually been proved in Courts of Law, which is far more than can be said for most scientific theories.[4]

Through many years of careful and painstaking research, the famous Dr. J. B. Rhine, of Duke University, and Dr. S. G. Soal of London,* have done their utmost to prove the reality of thought-transmission and other mental phenomena statistically and scientifically; and have succeeded in doing so to the satisfaction of most people with open minds and common-sense who have studied their researches. But even the name Extra Sensory Perception (ESP) has not made mental phenomena acceptable or respectable to the Scientific Establishment, for the reasons given earlier, especially the fact that mental phenomena are not repeatable at will.

There are good reasons for this which have so far escaped the notice of those who laugh at this research. The first is

* Senior Lecturer in Pure Mathematics, Queen Mary College, University of London.

that Nature designed the Universe without consulting our chemists and physicists and pays no attention whatever to their arbitrary requirements; she imposes her own rules and conditions for the study of her various phenomena. One of these is that, since thought interacts with thought, hostile, arrogant or ultra-critical thoughts can wreck sensitive experiments in mental phenomena as easily as light can fog a photographic film. An open-minded, observant but modest and sympathetic attitude of mind is as essential to research into mental phenomena as a darkroom is to photographic research. A hostile, know-it-all approach gets nowhere.

This has had some indirect confirmation from some brilliant research by Dr. Robert Rosenthal, of Harvard, who has shown that the bias—in other words, thoughts—of an experimenter can influence the behaviour of laboratory rats.[5] He has found that experimenters who have been *led to believe* that their rats are bright will get better results with their animals than experimenters who have been assured that their rats are dull, even though there is no known difference between the rats themselves.

In fairness to Dr. Rosenthal and to protect his reputation, it should be emphasized that *he* does *not* suggest that thought-transmission is the explanation. But his experimental results coincide with the well-known effects of thought on horses and dogs; and his research offers the first *statistical* confirmation that human attitudes—or thought—can affect animals.

If the mental attitude of a scientist can affect the performance of rats, it is easy to see that it could have devastating effects on some sensitive person experimenting with delicate mental phenomena. With so much criticism and derision of such research it is no wonder that experiments are rarely repeatable at will.

4

Confirmation that thought has field properties was provided some years ago by—of all things—some remarkable Russian research, which was made available to the West by a hilarious episode.

About 1959 a French publication published a story that

the United States Navy was using ESP to communicate with submarines at sea—which conjured up some diverting pictures of Admirals concentrating like crazy. Whether the Navy actually tried such experiments has never been officially disclosed as far as this reporter knows; if they did, it is hard to believe that it would not have become known by now, because such things are apt to leak out in Washington, especially at those times when the Congress is being asked for more money for research.

In any event, this French story flicked Communist pride on the raw and stimulated the Soviet Government to prove to the world that even Marxist-materialism was not behind American 'Imperialism' in parapsychological research. They accordingly permitted the publication of a work entitled 'Experiments in Mental Suggestion'[6] by Professor L. L. Vasiliev, Professor of Physiology in the University of Leningrad, with the official *imprimatur* of the Editorial Council of the University.

Nobody, of course, in the Scientific Establishments of the West paid the slightest attention to this important work— to them mental suggestion seemed suspect and anything by a Russian no doubt seemed doubly suspect. So the book might have been ignored but for the perception, enterprise and industry of two people in England—Anita Kohsen and C. C. L. Gregory—who had started an 'Institute for the Study of Mental Images': *

Realizing the immense significance of Dr. Vasiliev's work, this talented pair had it translated into English at the Institute, had the translation checked and approved by Dr. Vasiliev and then, with their own hands, set up 178 large pages of small type, printed them and bound the copies.

As these publishers rightly say: 'The book is unique— there is nothing comparable to it in the West.' It describes 'a remarkable scientific achievement—a book representing some 40 dedicated years, not only of one prominent scientist but of a whole team of collaborators—physicists, psychiatrists, engineers, physiologists, biologists and others. . . . The work

---

* Mr. Gregory subsequently died in a tragic accident and the Institute, most unfortunately, no longer operates. Quotations by kind permission of Mrs. A. Gregory.

is of the highest scientific calibre, experiments being described in such a way as to lend themselves to repetition, verification and citation of possible objections. Again and again criticisms were accepted, new methods devised, fresh subjects selected and experiments repeated.'

This work started as far back as 1921 and, at first, was officially encouraged by the Soviet Government. About 1937, however, it became clear that mental influencing does occur, that it is not impeded by distance, seems to have no connection with electromagnetic radiation and cannot be explained by physics. This seems to have worried the Marxist-materialists because the book was shelved—and probably suppressed—until 1959 when the ban was lifted in order to show the world that Russia was ahead of the United States in this work which, as a matter of fact, she still is.

It is impossible to summarize this technical, scholarly, and comprehensive book, packed with fascinating information. But to read it is to realize that Professor Vasiliev was a great scientist. He was open-minded, modest in his claims, receptive to criticism, scrupulously fair and meticulously careful in his experimental techniques—he went to unusual lengths to eliminate all chances of error or misconception. A brief description, however, of some of his work and findings is sufficient to show its importance from our point of view.

To determine the reality and nature of mental suggestion Professor Vasiliev adopted the plan of having a 'sender' make *purely mental* suggestions to a 'percipient' in another room to fall asleep or to wake up. By most ingenious arrangements and devices, it was made impossible for the 'percipient' to know if or when the mental suggestion had been made or for the 'sender' to know if his suggestion had had effect. But Professor Vasiliev and his colleagues had means of knowing when the mental suggestion was made, whether it was successful and how long it took to have its effect—this was sometimes almost instantaneous and sometimes, on the average, between under a minute and two and one-half minutes.

They were soon able to establish beyond doubt that *a suggestion or thought in one mind can produce an effect across space in another—a classic demonstration that thought has field properties.*

They also found that the distance between 'sender' and 'percipient' made no appreciable difference either in the effect or in the time involved. A 'percipient' in Sebastopol—roughly a thousand miles from Leningrad in a straight line—fell asleep or woke up in response to mental suggestions from Leningrad just as quickly and easily as when only two rooms away.

At one time it was supposed that thought-transmission is some kind of electromagnetic radiation. To find out whether this was so, Professor Vasiliev shut up the 'sender' in an air-tight lead chamber, its lid fitting into a trough of mercury and the whole carefully grounded. Sometimes the 'percipient' was also enclosed in a grounded metal chamber. These precautions did not weaken the effects of mental suggestion in any way.

Professor Vasiliev points out that this careful shielding eliminated all possibility of any electromagnetic radiations except 'in the region of radiation with a shorter wave (Röntgen or gamma-rays) which is improbable, or alternatively in the region of kilometre waves, or of static electric fields. However, the possibility of these last two factors playing a part also is hardly feasible'.

In his concluding paragraphs he confines himself to this modest statement:

'Of course everything that exists in the universe is not as yet understood. Now micro-fields are being discovered not exceeding the boundaries of the atom: could one not suppose that sooner or later a new macro-field will be discovered which will go beyond the boundaries of atoms and engulf the surrounding space?

'Some outstanding foreign scientists are already heading in this direction of research. For instance, Pascal Jordan, the German physicist and Nobel Prize winner, and Dr. B. Hoffman, a former collaborator of Einstein, think that a gravitational field seems to have some similarity with the force which transmits telepathic information, in that both act at a distance and penetrate all obstacles. . . .'

It will be noticed that Professor Vasiliev says flatly that *thought acts at a distance and penetrates all obstacles,* and is justified because his experimental techniques eliminated any possibility of other factors, such as sight or sound. He obtained his results with *pure thought alone*; and he found its effects were not diminished by distance or impeded by metal screening.

Other reasons apart, then, Professor Vasiliev's experimental results alone justify us in saying that thought acts like a field. And it would seem that, in reaching this conclusion, we are in the distinguished company of Dr. Pascal Jordan, Dr. B. Hoffman and Professor Vasiliev himself.

Though the latter doubts whether any known form of electromagnetic energy is involved in thought-transmission, from our point of view it does not matter either way. For if, one day, someone discovers some form of electromagnetic radiation associated with thought-transmission, that will merely be additional evidence that thought has field properties.

5

Once again we have run into something so new that not only does it have no short name but also no name at all. So, for convenience and to avoid confusion, it is up to us to coin a short title for 'a field in space originating with—or the result of—a thought which can produce effects at a distance without any visible intervening means on any person or object which is receptive to its force or influence'.

This pompous mouthful, it is suggested, can be reduced to 'thought-field' or 'T-field' for short.

This—it is freely admitted—is not euphonious and lacks the dignity befitting a description of an important natural phenomenon. But as we have to refer to thought acting as a field, no more suitable or succinct title suggests itself. A possible alternative, 'mind-field', must be rejected because mind is so often confused with the brain; and 'mind-field' might also be confused with the unpleasant devices of both World Wars. So 'T-fields' must do, unless or until someone can suggest something more suitable and elegant.

Before we consider what T-fields have to do with our four questions we must examine two of their properties. As we noted earlier, the fields known to physics come in all sizes from the infinitely-minute fields within the atom to the vast gravitational fields of space. And man-made fields have the same property.

For example, the electromagnetic field produced by a miniaturized radio-transmitter originates within the very small dimensions of the circuit but can extend an enormous distance in space.

We can see that T-fields can do the same thing. The T-fields, for instance, produced by Dr. Vasiliev's 'senders' originated within their brains—perhaps in only a small part of them—but could extend a thousand miles to Sebastopol.

A far more remarkable—and, from our point of view important—property of T-fields is that they can attach themselves to—or, if you prefer, localize themselves in—*any kind* of matter of any shape or size.

Though not recognized by science, this phenomenon has been known—and used—since early times. For it is the basis of the ancient customs of 'blessing' material objects or of putting a 'curse' on them. If, often, neither seem very effective, that does not prove that thoughts cannot be impressed on matter but merely that the thoughts were not strong enough to do good or ill to some tough character, perhaps because the blesser or curser did not know the proper technique.

It is not necessary, however, to be blessed or cursed to observe this phenomenon. One of its commonest forms are the thoughts of horror or despair impressed on the structure of a building in which some murder or tragedy has taken place. These powerful thoughts seem to saturate the building materials and to last indefinitely; and it is not necessary to have any special 'psychic' powers to sense them. Years after the tragedy, many visitors, who know nothing about it, will feel a sense of depression or uneasiness as soon as they walk into the building.

Many a real-estate-agent, trying to sell an apparently 'desirable property' must have been puzzled and disappointed when clients exclaimed: 'Ugh! Let's get out of here! This place gives me the willies!'

Sensitive people—more common than might be supposed —can get complete mental pictures, rather like motion-pictures, of the events that caused the T-fields to become associated with the building; and this uncomfortable gift is by no means confined to professional 'mediums'. Long ago, this reporter knew an 'amateur'—a lady of the highest integrity and with great humour and commonsense—who could not avoid 'seeing' past events in buildings about which she— and often the owners—knew nothing. Though she often found this involuntary aptitude embarrassing, horrifying and distressing and would have been glad to 'switch it off' if she had been able to, she made the best of it by confirming the accuracy of her mental pictures from local records, whenever possible.

From our point of view it is significant that this phenomenon is independent of the *size* of the material object on which the T-field is impressed—a small ring or jewel serves just as well to give a sensitive person a complete mental picture of past events associated with former owners—events which of course, do not have to be unpleasant to be recorded.

Here is an important clue to various problems: for instance, if a small jewel can 'anchor' a T-field representing a whole series of past events, it is easy to see how the cells of our brains can serve to 'anchor'—or localize—the T-fields of our thoughts or memories. And since T-fields—as Professor Vasiliev has demonstrated—can penetrate mental screens and exist in space on their own, we would logically expect them to be quite unaffected by the constant changes in the material of the brain.

A T-field is an elusive, shapeless, timeless thing, independent of matter and able to travel through space. It seems rational to assume, then, that before we can use it in the process of conscious thinking it has to be 'pinned down' or 'anchored' to something. In thinking, too, we often have to use our memories in a definite sequence by means of the mysterious 'scanning' mechanism of the brain. To make this process possible, it seems reasonable to suppose that the T-fields have to be anchored in a definite arrangement in a three-dimensional structure. That seems to be the function of the brain cells with their elaborate circuitry of nerves. At the same time, their intake of oxygen and ceaseless metabolism provides the energy needed to keep the circuits operating.

6

As the reader was warned to expect at the outset, our trail has led us to an unorthodox clue, for which there is no formal experimental support and about which relatively little has been written. This ability of thought to attach itself to any kind of matter does not attract much interest, even among parapsychologists. They know the phenomenon by the unfortunate name of 'psychometry' and accept its reality but do not regard it as important because, no doubt, they are not concerned with its biological implications.

Fortunately, this phenomenon is relatively easy to verify and any interested reader can do this for himself. If he cannot personally sense T-fields from objects he is almost certain to find someone who can among his friends. The writer cannot do it but has several friends who can; one of them tried the morning after hearing about the phenomenon for the first time and was immediately successful.

It does not seem to matter much whether the object is held in the hands or pressed against the forehead—the writer has seen both methods used successfully. The essential requirement—and the most difficult—is to relax completely and to exclude extraneous thoughts—and, as with most things of this kind, both practice and patience are necessary. Otherwise, there is no problem about arranging experiments which exclude all possibility of previous knowledge, thought-transmission or self-deception.*

---

* Some interesting examples of this phenomenon have been described by Geraldine Cummins—a talented author and investigator, who has long enjoyed the highest reputation among the many important people who have been familiar with her researches.

Miss Cummins has found that if two letters by different writers have been kept in close contact for a time, the T-field impressed by the writer with the most powerful personality can sometimes partially be transferred to the other letter and sensed from it by a sensitive. This interesting phenomenon—which the writer has not seen reported by any other research worker—is analogous to that of 'magnetic transference': unless certain technical precautions are taken a recording on one magnetic tape can be partly transferred to another tape held in close proximity for a long time. In the case of T-fields, the transference seems to depend more on their relative strength than on the duration of their proximity. (Cummins, Geraldine, *Unseen Adventures*. London: Rider and Company, 1951.)

Such experiments should—but most probably will not—be made by biologists and biochemists because the ability of T-fields to anchor themselves in any kind of matter gets them off several painful hooks by providing solutions to some of their most embarrassing problems.

DNA fans, for instance, tell us that the DNA molecule carries 'information' but frankly admit that they have no idea how it got the 'information' it is supposed to carry. They are also at a loss to explain what they call 'communications channels', still less the way in which supposed 'molecular messengers' carry 'information' to the cells, give them 'instructions' and see that these are carried out.

Just as they seem to ignore the existence of L-fields, these theorists do not seem to remember the constant changes of the materials of the body. Perhaps wisely, because this embarrassing fact makes their notions even harder to swallow.

It is difficult enough to believe that a molecule can carry 'information' or pass on 'instructions' to another molecule—nobody has ever found one molecule chatting to another. But it is even harder when we know that the molecules of the body are highly-unstable and constantly being torn down and replaced. And, since this is so, what we are being asked to believe is, in effect, this:

A complex molecule, due for replacement, somehow remembers to 'communicate' the 'information' it has been carrying, before it is torn down, to a fresh molecule which will carry on its duties. In some mysterious manner the dying molecule passes on this deathbed message to the younger generation: 'Look, fella, I'm being phased out and am headed for the john! Don't forget that your job is to see that this baby we're building has red hair! Be seeing you in the sewer—take it easy now!'

Unless we like fantasy as an 'escape', is it not easier to believe that heredity is 'all done by fields'? L-fields, as we know, have organizing qualities—that, in fact, is their job—and can come in all sizes. So they can ride herd on the smallest molecule or gene and since they can act across space can do some 'communicating'.

Since all human bodies, however, have the same general design and the same mechanisms, it may well be that the

L-fields only supply the standard mass-production blue-prints for the whole body and for all its standard sub-assemblies.

T-fields, on the other hand can carry any aspect of thought, whether it be designs, plans, organization or just plain information; and they could anchor themselves to a gene as easily as to a brain-cell. Thus they could supply individual 'custom features' by modifying the appropriate L-field which, as we shall see, they can do. To T-fields, too, which can produce effects over great distances, any 'communication' that might be needed across the length and breadth of the body would be no problem at all; and so T-fields may supplement the L-fields in the body's communication system.

As far, then, as the mechanism of physical heredity is concerned we have two choices: We can either believe that it is a field mechanism, because fields are known to exist, have the right qualifications for the job and are compatible with the trend of modern physics. Or we can believe—with the DNA fans—that it is all done by molecules. These certainly exist but their qualifications for the job are—at present, at least—purely imaginary.

In short—it is not unfair to say—the choice is between fact and fancy.

CHAPTER FIVE

More Clues

'Nature does nothing without purpose.'

1

Some other properties of thought or T-fields offer us some useful clues to our four questions.

One of these is that a T-field can influence or over-ride the organizing L-field of the body—as mentioned in the previous chapter. And perhaps the best-known evidence of this is the lowly Executive Ulcer.

As far too many people are painfully aware, anxiety about a falling sales-curve, about how to meet the next payroll or even about the probable reactions of the Internal Revenue Service to some borderline 'business expenses' can so disrupt the organization of an executive's L-field that an ulcer develops.

Since the earliest days of medicine, too, wise doctors have realized that the patient's attitude of mind has a lot to do with his general health. A powerful 'will to live' can sometimes reverse the medical probabilities while patients with a negative, despondent outlook may die when there is no physical reason why they should. This happened to some American prisoners with low morale during the Korean War.

In the East, especially, there are some who know the technique of withdrawing the 'will to live' when, for some reason, they have had enough of life and wish to die; though in perfect physical health, they can lie down and die in a few hours—a far less painful and messy way of leaving this life than the Japanese *hara-kiri*. In other words, by some mental process, they can neutralize the powerful L-field.

In India, years ago, this reporter found a spectacular and

well-authenticated case of this kind—but that is another story. Unfortunately he was unable to learn the technique employed, which would be useful to those in the West who do not want to be kept alive, as a burden to their families, by over-enthusiastic doctors.

In recent times, the effects of thought on health have been dignified with the title of 'psychosomatic symptoms', which has helped to get them accepted by modern medicine and to become quite fashionable.

As a by-product of this enthusiasm, modern pediatricians and modern mothers are beginning to re-discover something their ancestors always knew: that new-born babies benefit physically from love, while unwanted babies do not make such good progress. A mother's love, in other words, can invigorate the infant's L-field.

Some Eastern *fakirs* are able to suppress bleeding and—apparently—pain by some purely mental process, as this writer once was able to observe on two separate occasions in —of all places—London, England. He was assigned by his newspaper to witness the demonstrations of two rival *fakirs* and took with him a doctor to ensure that there was no medical hocus-pocus.

Closely surrounded by the Press, the *fakirs* lay half-naked on beds of nails, ran hatpins right through their cheeks, and one even stuck a knife through the fleshy part of the throat. In no case was there any sign of blood and, apparently, the demonstrators felt no pain. The doctor was able to certify that the *fakirs* were actually doing what they seemed to be doing and that there was no blood before—nauseated by the demonstration—he headed for the nearest bar. The reporter, feeling as sick as the doctor, would have liked to join him but felt it was better to see things through to the end than to incur the contempt of the Managing Editor.

Less nauseating and more scientific evidence of the influence of thought on the L-field is provided by the effect of hypnosis—the thought of one person—on the *physical structure of the eye* of another person, of which the writer has found two reports:

Dr. Milton H. Erickson, America's foremost authority on hypnosis, hypnotized a young man afflicted with acute shortsightedness and 'regressed' him to the age of eight—an age at which he had not needed glasses to read. In this condition of regression he was able to read books held at the wrong distance and to thread fine needles without either glasses or eyestrain.[1]

In some careful and ingenious experiments, too, Dr. Irwin M. Strosberg and Dr. Irving Vics found that they could produce *measurable physiological changes* in the eye by hypnosis.[2]

But perhaps the most important evidence that thought *directly* influences the L-field is provided by the remarkable experiments[3] of Dr. Leonard J. Ravitz, Jr., whom Dr. Burr has described as his 'most brilliant pupil'.

As already noted in Chapter 2 Dr. Ravitz has discovered that hypnosis produces voltage changes in the human L-field and that the actual depth of hypnosis can be measured by observing changes in the voltage-gradient with a recording voltmeter.

Though this discovery has so far been ignored, it is obviously of great importance to the understanding and study of mental illness. From our point of view, it provides completely objective, purely electronic evidence that thought can affect the organizing L-field of the body.

It might be argued that the psychosomatic effects described above were the result of thought acting directly on the physical organism. But nobody has ever found that thought can influence chemical reaction or an electric current. On the other hand, Dr. Ravitz has shown that it *can* affect an L-field. It seems reasonable to suppose, then, that thought can only act on the body through the L-field. In other words, L-fields are the intermediary 'mechanism' of psychosomatic symptoms.

As we follow our trail, it will be noticed that it leads us still further away from purely mechanical, chemical or particle explanations of life. For we have found not only that we are controlled by intangible electromagnetic fields but also that these can be modified—and sometimes overridden—by the even less tangible power of thought.

In short, L-fields—Nature's 'blue-prints'—can be changed by man's thoughts.

2

Another property of T-fields is their stability and permanence.

Most of us can remember hazily only a few events of early childhood. But hypnotic—and, sometimes, psychiatric—techniques can dredge up most detailed memories of our earliest years.

Undoubtedly the most striking evidence that the T-fields located in our brains—which represent our memories—are both permanent and detailed is provided by the astonishing experiments of the eminent neurosurgeon, Dr. Wilder Penfield, when he was Director of the Montreal Neurological Institute at McGill University.

In the course of essential brain-operations, Dr. Penfield electrically stimulated the cortex, with the patients under a local anaesthetic only and fully conscious of what was going on. When he touched the electrodes to various points on the surface of the cortex, patients would 're-live' forgotten episodes of the past, complete with sights and sounds and in perfect time sequence.

Though fully aware of the present and of the fact that they were on the operating table, patients seemed actually to *re-experience* the past, moment by moment and 'at time's own unchanged pace'. This seemed to be much more vivid and real than just a memory. And sometimes the same 'record' could be played again by touching the electrode to the same spot.

Dr. Penfield has explained that the area of the brain around the electrode is put out of action but the electrical stimulus at that point activates other parts of the brain and brings past experiences back to conscious recall.

Then, as Dr. Penfield puts it,[4] 'the subject re-lives a period of the past although he is still aware of the present. Movement goes forward again as it did in that interval of time that has now been, by chance, revived and *all of the elements of his previous consciousness seem to be there*—sights, sounds, interpretations, emotion.' (Our italics.)

As we shall see, it is significant from our point of view

that the past experiences 're-lived' in this way were 'not particularly important ones'.

'One conclusion seems to me to be safe,' Dr. Penfield has written.[5] 'There is within the brain a ganglionic record of past experience which preserves the individual's current perception in astonishing detail. *This record, one may assume, is to serve some subsequent purpose.*' (Our italics.)

In a later work[6] he wrote:

'The experiential responses of the flash-back variety were, for the most part, quite unimportant moments in the patient's life—standing on a street corner, hearing a mother call a child, taking part in a conversation, listening to a little boy as he played in the yard. If these unimportant minutes of time were preserved in the ganglionic recordings of these patients, *why should it be thought that any experience in the stream of consciousness drops out of the ganglionic record.*

'When, by chance, the neurosurgeon's electrode activates past experience, *that experience unfolds moment by moment.* This is a little like the performance on a wire-recorder or a strip of cinematographic film on which are registered all those things of which the individual was once aware—the things he selected for his attention in that interval of time. Absent from it are the sensations he ignored, the talk he did not heed.

'Time's strip of film runs forward, never backward, even when resurrected from the past. It seems to proceed again at time's own unchanged pace.... As long as the electrode is held in place, the experience of a former day goes forward. There is no holding it still, no turning back, no crossing with other periods. When the electrode is withdrawn it stops as suddenly as it began....

'Consciousness, "forever flowing" past us makes no record of itself *and yet the recording of its counterpart within the brain is astonishingly complete.*' (Our italics.)

In a recent lecture,[7] Dr. Penfield said:

'The engram of the stream of consciousness is the sequence record of what came within the focus of man's attention—his awareness, his thoughts and his emotions. No one can prove that the record is complete for the whole of man's conscious past, although it is difficult to conceive why it should be discontinuous.'

Dr. Penfield's classic experiments show that every experience of which we have ever been aware is preserved in the 'astonishingly complete' records within the brain, despite the ceaseless metabolism and changes of brain-material. And Nature, the supreme organizer, does nothing without reason. So, as Dr. Penfield so wisely observes: 'This record, one may assume, is to serve some subsequent purpose'—a purpose we shall shortly attempt to discover.

As we found in the previous chapter, it is not only in the cells of the brain that records of the past—in the form of T-fields—can be preserved indefinitely. Sensitive people, by holding an object or entering a building hundreds or even thousands of years old, can 're-live' episodes of the past, probably in much the same way as Dr. Penfield's patients.

Located in the brain, then, or in other kinds of matter, T-fields seem to last indefinitely, which need not surprise us because that is a well-known property of fields. Certain magnetic materials in the earth's crust, for instance, have preserved their fields for untold ages while pulses from 'radio-stars' have preserved the pattern of their fields in the millions of years they have taken to travel to us across space.

3

We have become so accustomed to thinking of thoughts and memories as a part or product of the brain that, admittedly, it is hard to realize that the brain is merely a marvellous mechanism which is *used* by our thoughts and memories and that these can exist apart from it. In much the same way, a programmer can use a computer without being part of it or having to live in it.

A lot has been written in recent years, too, which gives the impression that computers will soon duplicate all the mysteries of the human mind and that, with a little more 'sophisticated' circuitry, our technicians will soon be able to produce the equivalent of the human brain. Oddly enough, these optimistic predictions seem to ignore the part played by the human programmer, without whose thoughts even the most wonderful computer is completely useless. And they forget, too, that no computer could work at all if all its material was constantly changing.

Before we go any further, therefore, perhaps we should briefly consider some facts about the brain which are often overlooked in the current hoopla about 'cybernetics' and computers.

Modern experiments have shown that mind and memory are not only unaffected by the constant replacement of brain material: they can also survive the actual removal of large sections of the brain. To quote another work of Sir Charles Sherrington: [8]

'Today the surgeon removes large areas of the cortex of the brain—the cortex is the region where brain and mind meet— from *conscious patients without their noticing difference or change.*' (Our italics.)

It is also known that, sometimes, when a part of the brain is damaged, another part can take over its duties—an indication that brain functions—with some important exceptions —do not depend on any special area of brain material.

This fact was strikingly demonstrated, in some famous experiments on rats, as long ago as 1929, by the well-known neuropsychologist, Dr. K. S. Lashley.[9] He found that the ability of rats to learn was reduced roughly in proportion to the *amount* of brain material that he removed; and that it made no difference from which part of the brain the material was taken away.

Moreover, Dr. Lashley—and also two later writers—[10] came to the conclusion that learning—that is, memory— depends not on local differentiations in the structure of the brain but on some 'general dynamic' or some 'dynamic principle' of the entire cerebral system. This supports our concept that thought has field properties because a 'dynamic' implies forces in action in space.

Until all this was known, it was natural to confuse effect with cause and to regard thought as the product of the brain and nervous system. But now it is clear that thought is the 'craftsman' and that the physical brain is merely its 'tool'.

To the German Intelligence of World War II we owe an analogy which helps to visualize a T-field of a memory, localized in a brain-cell. As some readers will remember, German photographic experts devised a method of reducing a whole page of closely-typed information to a 'microdot' about the size of the periods printed on this page. These tiny microfilms were stuck on a harmless letter under the stamp or stuck in some pre-arranged position on the envelope, and to any censor who noticed them they seemed like small fly-specks—until the F.B.I. found out about them.

We can picture the T-fields representing our memories— or all the bits and pieces of information we learn in our lives—as the equivalent of 'microdots' attached to our brain-cells, occupying negligible physical space but carrying a vast amount of information. And just as the German 'microdots' were 'blown-up' in Berlin to the original page-size, so the T-fields in our brains can be enlarged to any size required by the 'screen' of the mind.

Sometimes these mental pictures can actually reproduce themselves on a photographic film which, when developed, displays a recognizable image, occasionally one of remarkable clarity and detail.

This was first demonstrated as long ago as 1910 by Professor T. Fukurai, of Kohyassan University. He found that certain people can concentrate on a design or picture and, *by thought alone*, transfer a clear reproduction to a *sealed* photographic plate, without the aid of light or a lens.[11]

Since that time others have not only duplicated Professor Fukurai's experiments but also have produced some interesting variations of this phenomenon. This reporter has examined some of these but it would take too long to describe them here.

A few years ago, Dr. Jule Eisenbud, M.D., found a man with the ability to transfer mental pictures to film and, with dedicated perseverance, carried out a most careful and scientific examination, described in his much-discussed book, *The World of Ted Serios*.[12]

Nobody seems to know for certain *how* a thought can produce a chemical change in the silver-bromide molecules of a photographic emulsion. But Dr. Ravitz' discovery that thought can affect the electromagnetic field of the body suggests at least a partial explanation. For if thought can affect one kind of electromagnetic field, no doubt it can affect other kinds. So it seems reasonable to suppose that a T-field imposed on a photographic film so modifies the *fields* of the silver-bromide molecules that an image can be developed.

This phenomenon, of course, dramatically confirms our conclusion that thought acts like a field because only a field could produce effects across the space between the 'concentrator' and the film and also penetrate the coverings in which the film is sealed, at the same time preserving a definite pattern. This is also interesting because it shows that T-fields can assume a design of definite physical dimensions, which can produce its counterpart within the dimensions of the film.

If, too, a 'mental microdot' can impress a 'blown-up' picture on the fields of silver-bromide molecules, it is easier to understand that it can affect the fields of other kinds of molecules in a jewel or in the material of a building. And although the resulting 'image' cannot be developed chemically it can be 'seen' by people with sufficient sensitivity.

This offers us another clue to the nature of thought: under certain circumstances, at least, thought can produce what chemists call a 'reversible reaction'. The thought of one person can produce an effect on matter, which can reproduce the original thought in the mind of another person, either directly or by means of an image on film.

To put it another way, thought can 'charge up' matter by modifying its fields, in much the same way as electricity can charge an automobile-battery by changing its chemistry. Just as the reversible chemical reactions of the battery return some of the electricity when we press the starter, so the reversible field-reactions of thought—so to speak—can cause matter to reproduce the thought that 'charged' it. But there is an important difference: matter never *seems* to lose its 'charge' however many people may sense it. An old jewel may have been worn by many people—an ancient building lived in by hundreds or visited by thousands—but the impressed T-fields *seem to* retain sufficient 'charge' to be 'seen' by a sensitive person. But this—as far as the writer knows—has neither been proved nor disproved.

All this suggests the way in which the T-fields of our thoughts or memories 'anchor' themselves to the 'moorings' of the brain-cells. Though the atoms and molecules of which they are composed are in a constant state of flux and change, each cell must have its tiny, permanent L-field to control this tearing down and building up. As Dr. Ravitz has shown that thought can measurably affect the overall L-field of the body, it is logical to assume that it can also affect the sub-fields of the cells. It is one of these tiny L-fields, then, that the T-fields must modify in some way, with a 'mental micro-dot', each time we consciously learn, remember or observe something.

No doubt Nature has designed these cells in such a way that their L-fields are specially receptive to this kind of 'charge', just as makers of the best modern batteries use chemicals in the cells which can most easily take and hold an electric charge.

Students of the brain tell us that, normally, during our lives we only 'charge up' a part of the huge battery of cells available in the brain. Nature seems to have provided a great surplus of 'moorings' to which to 'anchor' all the T-fields we are ever likely to form or need. It seems, too, that some have been provided for emergencies and—sometimes—can be taken over by existing T-fields if their former 'moorings' have been destroyed by brain-injuries.

4

It is accepted that certain areas of the brain are definitely linked with the senses of sight, speech, smell, hearing and taste and also with the control of various parts of the body. And if these areas are damaged, other parts of the brain can rarely if ever take over. But, as far as learning and memory are concerned, the experience of brain surgeons and the experiments of Dr. Lashley and others seems to show that as long as enough cells are left to 'charge up' it does not matter in which part of the brain they are located.

It is easy to see why this is so: our senses are an integral part of the physical equipment of the body; the controlling brain-cells must be permanently 'wired in', so to speak, to the whole system and, if they are damaged, the circuits cannot be transferred to other cells. But our thoughts and memories are not part of our standard physical equipment and are not permanently connected to the 'wiring' of the brain, though they can switch it on when necessary. So it does not matter in which part of the brain they are 'stored'— as long as there are enough cells for them to 'charge up'.

Some of the tragic patients in insane asylums may be able to use all their senses and move their limbs like the rest of us as these are a part of their physical equipment—all too often a distressingly healthy one. But they may be unable to learn or remember anything and seem to have lost the capacity to 'charge up' any of their cells.

To put this in another way, our senses have to be on the job continuously, in order to keep the body going and to protect it from injury. For this reason the controlling and interpretive cells of the brain must always be 'warmed up' and the wiring system permanently 'alive'. But our thoughts and memories are only used intermittently and are only brought out of storage up to consciousness as we need them. To use a military analogy, some of the cells are concerned with 'operations' and the others with records or intelligence.

Our senses often help us to 'pull' the files of memory. We see somebody's face and, with luck, that evokes the memory of his name. Something we taste may conjure up a picture of that cookie-jar we used to plunder when we were small. A whiff of perfume at a party may give a man a mental vision of that lovely girl he used to dance with years ago—the sense of smell, by the way, often seems the most effective trigger of memory. On the other hand, a mere memory 'out of the blue' may by itself stimulate others or a whole train of thought.

Whatever the stimulus that starts it, however, what is the *process* by which the files are pulled?* How do we match

* For a recent and authoritative discussion of this highly-technical subject see *Engrams in the Human Brain: Mechanisms of Memory* by Wilder Penfield. Gold Medal Lecture at the Royal Society of Medicine, London. April 4, 1968.

the sight of a face with a remembered name? How do we associate a printed word with the meaning we learned long ago? How do we interpret a series of sound frequencies reaching our ears as a familiar word or a favourite tune?

In the present state of our knowledge, we cannot find a complete answer to these questions. But all the clues we have assembled can give us at least a part of the answer.

We have seen that the human body is a complicated package of electromagnetic fields—from the sub-fields of organs, cells and molecules down to the fields within the atoms—all wrapped up in an overall, controlling L-field. We have seen that the latter 'knows', so to speak, what is happening in its component fields—a local abnormality can be detected in the field at a distance from the site of the trouble. Like any good organizer, in other words, the L-field keeps track of the entire organization.

We have seen that thought acts like a field and that T-fields representing specific memories can be 'anchored' to the brain cells by modifying their little L-fields. To this complicated package of T-fields we add every day of our lives as we read, meet or learn something new. It is an amazingly-assorted grab-bag of T-fields, representing anything from words we learned at school to something we saw on TV yesterday. This random assortment presents an even greater problem of organization than the organs and cells of the body, nicely fixed in standard arrangements, despite their changing chemistry.

And yet it is so well organized that it is available for instant use. When we want to say something, those words of which we formed T-fields in our schooldays 'spring to mind' without conscious effort. That episode we saw on TV yesterday recalled a whole bunch of memories of a similar programme a few years ago. We meet someone we hardly know but his face brings back immediate memories of what happened the time we last saw him.

Is it not obvious that all these thoughts and memories must be organized by something—by some 'general dynamic' as Dr. Lashley suggested—that can keep track of them and make them available for use? And since thought acts like a field, what *else* could organize them but an *overall controlling*

81

T-field, analogous to the overall L-field that organizes all the electromagnetic fields of the body?

This controlling, organizing T-field must, of course, *use* the cells and nerve-circuits of the brain to 'match-up' the messages from our senses with our memories. It must also use the mechanism of the brain to make our vocal chords and lips utter the words it wants spoken, to move our fingers if we want to type a letter or to move our arms and hands when we drive the car. But this T-field is *not* the brain—it merely uses the brain as we use various man-made mechanisms.

As the brain is part of our physical organization, its mechanism is under the immediate control of the L-field. But, for the brain, at least, the L-field is not the boss but the maintenance-man, analogous to the technicians who have to replace burnt-out tubes or transistors in computers, to keep them working for the benefit of those who use them.

There can be no doubt that the T-field is the boss in this instance because, as we saw earlier, it can sometimes control the L-field.

5

This sketchy—and doubtless incomplete*—outline is admittedly an intangible one. But, in these days, there is nothing impracticable or unscientific about intangibles. For science itself—as we have already noted—is more and more concerned with such intangible, invisible things as fields and waves. In concluding, then, that thought behaves like a field and can exist and function quite independently of matter, far from being 'far out', we are in harmony with the trend of physics.

Despite this, our conclusion will inevitably upset those who resist any suggestion that body and 'mind' are two separate things, for reasons which often seem more emotional

* A distinguished physician and psychiatrist reports that certain sensitives can 'see' clairvoyantly no less than three separate kinds of field associated with the human body. They tell her that the condition of these fields indicates the mental and physical condition of the patient. For an account of this research see *Breakthrough to Creativity—Your Higher Sense Perception* by Shafica Karagulla, M.D. Los Angeles, California, 90041, DeVorss and Co., Inc.

than rational. It is quite natural, of course, to want to explain everything in terms of what we already know; and biologists who have never studied thought want to explain it in terms of biology or those who have only studied computers want to explain it by computers.

Some of the purely emotional opposition to the separation of mind and body may be due to an addiction to the Theory of Evolution, because, if 'mind' is separate from body, it is hard to believe that it can be the *result* of *physical* evolution, even though it may have been influenced by it.

On the contrary, there are some good reasons for supposing that *mind and body have had entirely separate evolutions.*

One of these is that thought—the basis of mind—is non-physical and a field phenomenon. As all the fields we know about dominate matter—though they may be affected by it—it is most unlikely that a field can be the product of physical evolution.

Another is that since thought can exist in—and function across—space, without any association with matter, there is no reason to suppose that association with matter is essential for its evolution.

Yet another is that all human bodies—whether of aborigines or University Presidents—are strikingly similar; and even freaks are rare. Moreover, as one authority quoted earlier said, the general design has not changed significantly in 100,000 years. But all human 'minds' are different; and the difference runs the whole gamut from an Einstein or a Shakespeare to a hopeless moron.

Similarity and variety cannot be produced by the same process; Hart Schaffner and Marx do not make suits in the same way as Savile Row. Though physical evolution, then, may explain our standardized bodies, it cannot possibly account for our 'custom-built' minds.

For this reason, *it is evident that body and mind do not evolve at the same rate and therefore cannot evolve concurrently.*

But, at present, it is still unfashionable to imagine 'mind' or thought as something apart from matter. In certain circles, in fact, convention has instilled such a terror of suggesting that matter and 'spirit' are separate realities that even the word 'purpose' is shunned in case it might be thought to have spiritual implications. Such gobbledegook as 'goal-motivated activity' is considered safer and more fashionable than 'purpose'.

Our conclusion, then, that thought is a field phenomenon apart from matter may not disturb physicists but will certainly stir up other hornets' nests. This investigation, however, is concerned with facts, not fashions and is trying to trace a new trail; and hornets are a normal hazard of new trails.

Hornets, too, are always interesting to observe.

CHAPTER SIX

University of Earth

He never wasted a leaf or a tree.
Do you think He would squander souls?
—*Kipling*[1]

1

Taken together, the assorted clues we have dug up can now suggest a more complete answer to our first question, *What are we?*

Human beings are complicated packages of at least two kinds of fields—electromagnetic life-fields and thought-fields —associated with a complex physical structure, the materials of which are constantly changing. The pattern and organization of the body is maintained by the L-fields which, however, can sometimes be modified or overruled by the T-fields.

Since the cells and molecules of the body are always being torn down and rebuilt, *only the fields are stable and enduring.*

Of the two kinds of field, the electromagnetic L-fields are common to the whole human race, because all human bodies are organized in the same general pattern. But the thought-fields, which are composed of individual memories and experience, are peculiar to each individual and exclusively his own.

In the previous chapter we visualized these as an assortment of little T-fields, associated with brain-cells, organized and controlled by an overriding T-field, which embraces the lot.

That's us—the essential, individual part of us that makes each one of us different from everyone else. That is what some people refer to as the 'soul' or the 'spirit' and others may call the 'mind', 'personality' or 'ego'. But, as all these

85

terms may have different shades of meaning for different people, perhaps we should avoid confusion by finding another word to describe the individual, controlling T-field; and *entity* seems the most suitable. Webster defines *entity* as: 'A being; especially a thing which has reality and distinctness of being either in fact or in thought.'

Few will quarrel with that definition of the individual part of us. Most people accept that their 'personalities' are real enough and, from earliest childhood, all of us are conscious of a separate, individual identity.

'Is then soul annihilable?' asked Shelley.[2]

'Yet one of the properties of the animal soul is consciousness of identity. If this is destroyed, in consequence, the soul (whose essence this is) must perish but, as I conceived ... that nothing can be annihilated ... then do I suppose ... that neither will soul perish.'

Though Shelley wrote this long before the modern discoveries we have examined, his poet's insight led him straight to two important truths: first, that individuality and consciousness of it are the essence of the entity and, second, that nothing can be annihilated.

Modern physics has endorsed Shelley in less poetic language with its Law of the Conservation of Mass and of Energy—in other words, matter and energy can neither be created nor destroyed but only altered in form. Nuclear physics has shown that matter can sometimes be converted into energy—in accordance with Einstein's famous equation $E = MC^2$—and sometimes energy can be converted into matter. But nothing can ever be annihilated and all the bits and pieces of mass and energy in the Universe will always add up to the same total.

Fields are an integral part of matter and energy—the organizing factor—and it is an axiom that no integral part of an unannihilable whole can cease to exist. So, though fields may change their form, they cannot be annihilated. *And this must apply to any kind of field, including the fields of thought.*

We shall find other reasons why this must be so as we

go along; and, in Chapter 8 we shall see that thought-fields are a manifestation of the Ultimate Reality and therefore imperishable.

In the case of the entity, the countless little T-fields of memory of which it is made up are more than an integral part: they are its very essence and, by the axiom stated above, cannot be annihilated. So, since laws of various kinds are fashionable nowadays, we should formulate the 'Law of the Conservation of the Entity and of its Memories'. Or, in plain English, *individuality is indestructible*.

We can find support for this quite apart from the laws of physics. We have only to look around to find that Nature conserves everything and wastes nothing. Trees and plants die and decompose to furnish nourishment for new growth. All the materials of which our bodies are composed are eventually returned to the earth to furnish materials for other living forms—as we have already noted. This was once brought home to this reporter in a horrible way when—assigned to cover a factory explosion—he found himself walking through a field littered with fragments of bone and flesh, too small and scattered to be gathered and buried. But he realized that these would soon be absorbed to nourish fresh grass, on which cattle could graze and that their milk would nourish babies.

If Nature is so economical with mere matter, why suppose that her more complex creations—fields of life and thought-fields—should be any exception to the general rule?

We have seen from the experiments of Dr. Wilder Penfield and also from the findings of psychiatry and hypnotism that our memories even of trivial things are preserved in 'astonishing detail' even though we do not *consciously* remember them—this despite the fact that a part of our brains and bodies 'dies' every day. If Nature goes to all this trouble to 'conserve' even the unimportant components of the entity—through innumerable 'partial deaths' of brain and body—does it make sense to suppose that she throws away the whole lot, when the brain and body die completely?

This seems all the more improbable when we remember that fields of thought can exist and function in space, with no matter around and that—localized in jewels or buildings

—can apparently last for an indefinite time.

Whether we like it or not, then, all the evidence suggests that memories of everything we have learned or experienced, pleasant or unpleasant, are conserved in an amazingly-detailed permanent memory, which makes the 'memories' of even the most modern computers look like old-fashioned box-files. Which is another way of saying that the entity, with all its 'files', must continue to exist after the death of the body with which it was associated. And we shall find more evidence of this when we examine thought further.

2

If we find it hard to imagine permanent records of everything that we—and all the rest of the human race—have ever learned or experienced, we have only to remember that Nature revels in infinite variety and can handle unlimited detail and astronomical numbers. Even simple living forms of the same species often—if not always—display minor variations and, generally speaking, the more complex the form, the greater the variations. Even 'identical' twins at least have different finger-prints, as the F.B.I. has confirmed to the writer.

Nature must go to all this trouble because memories are the mainspring of the human personality. We, as individual personalities, are largely the product of what we have learned or experienced. Each of us is born, of course, with different qualities of mind and heart, which can be developed by the lessons of life. But we could not develop them at all without a memory with which to record and profit by our experience.

Even the most trivial experience or seemingly-unimportant remembered fact can make some contribution to the entity. We can sometimes *learn* more from an unimportant event than from an important one. Some minor episode—perhaps long in the past—may influence our judgement today. And we can never tell when some isolated memory of years ago may prove the key to a problem of tomorrow. A distant memory, for instance, of a casual and irrelevant conversation once enabled this writer to solve an urgent problem connected with radar just before the Battle of Britain. Or the memory of some minor mistake or mishap may avert a repetition on a larger scale. This, no doubt, is why our memories are preserved in 'astonishing detail'.

It goes without saying that if Nature preserves all the component memories of the entity she must also preserve the controlling entity as a whole because without this organizing T-field—which we have termed the entity—our memories could not be used.

Nature—we may assume—does nothing without purpose or, to be in the fashion, without 'goal-motivated activity', even if we cannot always discern what it is. And there would be no point in arranging for memories to be formed and preserved if they were not intended to be used.

It seems reasonable to deduce, then, that *the purpose of human life must be to develop the entity by experience. In short, we are alive to learn.*

Though our experiences have probably done more to make us what we are than we realize, many people must have accumulated a stock of knowledge and experience which cannot be fully used in their present lives. Lots of people die with a sense of 'unfinished business'—with the feeling that they could have accomplished more, if they had had more time. But as memory—which is thought 'crystallized' as a field—can exist apart from matter, there is no reason to suppose that any experience will be wasted but will be available for use in another existence. On the contrary, surely we are justified in assuming that economical Nature has arranged that no experience is wasted.

As far as this existence is concerned, we can observe that all men and women are born different, and, as they go through life and the more they learn by experience, the more different and individual they tend to become. In other words, the more they stock their entities with memories of experiences or knowledge, each in his own way, the more they develop their individuality—which serves Nature's enthusiasm for infinite variety.

So we can go a step further and deduce that the purpose of life is to *develop our own individuality by experience. We are alive not merely to learn but also to develop our individual potential to the utmost.*

It is obvious that we cannot do that—cannot fulfil Nature's plan—unless we have as much freedom as is possible without impairing the freedom of others. A police-state is no place to develop individuality. Nor is a welfare-state carried to the point where it destroys individual initiative, as so often happens at the present time.

We can assume, then, that *individual freedom is an essential part of Nature's plan*. And, since this is so, it cannot be a coincidence that the United States and the British Commonwealth, with their long traditions of freedom for the individual, achieved such unexampled heights of progress, prosperity and power. They have not tried to 'lick' Nature as the dictators have done; they have 'joined' her.

As we noted earlier, there are two sides to the coin of freedom. If Nature intends us to use our freedom to develop our individuality, she must also expect us to stand on our own feet and to take responsibility for our own acts. We have the freedom to profit by doing right but also the obligation to take the consequences of doing wrong. We cannot enjoy the one without the other.

Again it can be no coincidence that this was the virile, independent outlook of the pioneers who built the British Commonwealth and the United States. It is still the outlook of those who start new businesses, launch new inventions and risk new enterprises from which, if successful, thousands of Milquetoasts—dedicated to 'security' and afraid to make mistakes—will ungratefully derive their livelihood.

Nature's plan, then, is not so abstract as it might seem at first sight: it is so practical, in fact, that it creates jobs.

3

If we can accept that the individual entity with all its memories is conserved—immortal, if you prefer—and that the purpose of our present existence is to learn, we can see why life on this planet is neither so unfair nor disorganized as it often seems. We can see human affairs, with all their troubles, injustices and confusions, in their true perspective.

We can see that this planet is really a vast college, offering an infinite variety of courses, some tough, some relatively easy. We know from our school and college days that we can get more out of a tough course than an easy one—though the latter may be more fun. In later life we can usually learn more from trouble than from pleasure. Most of us have friends who have 'risen above' some tragedy or disaster and emerged finer, better and stronger people; every street and every village can show examples. On a wider scale, wars or disasters evoke endless examples of fortitude, bravery, and self-sacrifice for which peace and prosperity offer fewer opportunities.

Is not this sufficient evidence not only that this is Nature's purpose but also that it is achieved?

Since, therefore, the purpose of life is to develop individuality, we cannot expect to fulfill it only by easy or pleasant experiences. After all, in her experiments with other living forms, Nature subjects them to ruthless competition and, often, harsh environment and conditions. She has established the rule of 'tooth and claw' and, as the cigarette advertisements used to put it, 'Nature in the raw is seldom mild'. Similarly, the human entity could not develop in a Utopian environment of perpetual sweetness and light which offered no tests or challenges.

That, no doubt, is why man has freedom to learn from his own mistakes or from those of others, just as in any good college students are allowed freedom because it is good for their development. For the same reason, no doubt, Nature permits extensive 'hazing' in the form of wars, natural disasters and human disasters like a Hitler or a Stalin.

In the University of Earth, the students seem to have unlimited freedom. In the past twenty years, in fact, they have gained the freedom to destroy the whole campus with missiles and hydrogen bombs. If that happens, however, and if this planet becomes uninhabitable it need have no effect—except, perhaps, an emotional one—on the development of human entities because these, being non-physical cannot be destroyed by exploding matter and cannot be damaged by fall-out. And there is plenty of room in the Universe for the development of entities to be continued elsewhere, if necessary, because—as Professor Vasiliev and others have shown—

thought-fields can traverse space without attenuation or loss of identity.

No doubt the students of this University have the right to 'pursue' happiness. But, if they fail to catch it, they may really be getting more value out of this college life than some others. And since the students enroll with unequal qualifications, it is evident that the 'faculty' makes no attempt to guarantee equal success or happiness for everyone.

So it is idle to expect any quick or easy answer to our college examinations or to hope that our fellow-students—or the Government—can achieve for us what the 'faculty' does not attempt in this semester.

On the other hand, we can take comfort from the reflection that nothing we can learn at this University is either wasted or lost—that we *can* 'take it with us' in the limitless 'files' of the immortal entity.

For this reason we are not justified in saying that 'a young life has been wasted' when some boy or girl dies young; perhaps they have successfully passed all the examinations scheduled for them by Nature. There may be a profound truth in the ancient saying: 'Those whom the gods love, die young.'

A few weeks ago, a boy in his twenties—known to the writer—died a lingering, painful death from cancer. But he met his fate bravely, without complaint and even insisted on completing on his death-bed the work for his doctorate. Can we say that life was 'wasted' when he strengthened his will and his fortitude by the experience and was an inspiration to all his friends? Would it not be more accurate to say that he had passed his examinations earlier than most—and with flying colours?

Of those in the Armed Forces who so gallantly give their lives for their country, we can say with admiration—and envy—that they have passed the supreme test and have graduated, *summa cum laude*, from the University of Earth.

4

If, to us, there seem to be no rules in the University of Earth and no restraint on the conduct of the students, that is because we can only observe one brief semester in the long development of the human entity. But when we consider the ordered precision of the Universe and its exact and inexorable laws, we cannot seriously believe that Nature is so naïve as to have omitted to provide some checks and balances for human conduct, as she has done for everything else. But she is infinitely patient and, since the entity survives death, there is all eternity for these checks and balances to take effect.

In the final analysis, all 'wrong-doing'—which is a relative term—involves some interference with the freedom of others to live and enjoy their lives in their own way. Therefore, since freedom is Nature's purpose for man, all 'wrong-doing' is a breach of her laws.

No natural law that we know can be defied or broken with impunity, even if the penalty is sometimes long delayed. If we defy the law of gravity and walk over a cliff, the penalty is immediate. If we flout the obvious rules of health or take to drugs, patient Nature may take years to exact the inevitable penalties.

Whether the penalties for violating Nature's laws come fast or slow, then, there is no escape—and, as far as we can see, no appeal. We cannot seriously expect to bribe Nature to relax her universal laws for us. Nor—in all sanity—can we hope to hire a lawyer—or to cajole a Saint—to get us off. And, as with our laws, we may assume that 'ignorance of the law is no excuse.' If, then, individuals, groups or nations violate Nature's law of freedom by doing harm to others, we may be sure—from our experience of other natural laws— that they will incur some 'penalty', however long this may take.

From some of the clues we have assembled we can get at least a rough idea of the way in which this works:

1. As we have seen, hypnotism—the thought of another— can have powerful effects on us.

2. Psychosomatic medicine and also modern psychiatry have shown that our own thoughts and memories can harm even the tough, physical organization of our bodies.

3. In the course of the classic experiments described earlier, Professor Vasiliev established that the thoughts of the hypno-

tist can reach the mind of the percipient if the former merely holds a mental picture of the latter. *It is not necessary for the hypnotist to know where the percipient is.* Others have also found experimentally—in ways which would take too long to describe here—that thought can always find its target if the target is known.

4. As Professor Vasiliev—and others—have also found neither time nor distance make any difference to the effects of thought.

All this suggests that if our actions have aroused thoughts of anger or hatred in the minds of others we cannot evade them, wherever we may be, provided those we have wronged know what we look like. And to the immortal entity, of course, death offers no escape.

On the contrary, we would expect the thoughts of others to have far more direct and powerful effects on the entity itself than on the body, because the entity *is* thought. In other words, the entity is a 'sitting duck' for the bullets of thought—a *personal*, perpetual target for the destructive thoughts of those it has harmed.

Apart from the thoughts of others, our own remorse—if or when we are capable of feeling it—must also painfully affect our entities. This may apply not only when we have harmed others but also if we have harmed ourselves by flunking our courses in the University of Earth or even trying to 'drop out'. In such cases, too, we probably have to take the same kind of course again somewhere and somehow, because we cannot expect to flout Nature's purpose.* No student riots are likely to impress Nature.

As any good psychiatrist knows, our own thoughts can sometimes—and quite literally—'give us hell' in this present existence without waiting for a future one. For example, Jung tells a dramatic story of one of his patients, a murderess,

---

* Suicide can sometimes be regarded as 'dropping out'. *But by no means always.* For the writer has had personal knowledge of some suicides which were solely the result of sheer physical and nervous exhaustion from prolonged overwork. This exhaustion induced an overpowering depression.

In such cases—he believes—suicide should be regarded in the same light as death from some other purely physical cause, such as a heart-attack.

The writer has also known of suicides which were the result of courageous self-sacrifice and the desire to relieve others of a burden.

who had punished herself with an unbearable loneliness, even though—apparently—she felt no moral consciousness of having done wrong. So intense were her feelings that even animals shunned her, to make her loneliness even more bitter. Jung felt that criminals who evade human justice can sometimes punish themselves in this way.[3]

This prospect of an 'automatic hell' is not pleasant to contemplate, even for the petty crook or the selfish irresponsible. But, for a dictator who has brought death or suffering to millions or the leader who has deliberately misled a nation, the prospect is positively terrifying. For modern propaganda, press photography and TV make sure that the whole world has mental pictures of its public figures.

Ironically, in fact, modern propaganda methods employed by dictators and others to build their personal 'images' are multiplying the penalties they will suffer in the future, if they give cause to their followers to be angry with them. To this, a saying of Abraham Lincoln is particularly appropriate:

'In times like the present, men should utter nothing for which they would not willingly be responsible through time and eternity.'

This is even more desirable than in Lincoln's day when the faces of public men were not familiar to millions, when their audiences were often limited by the strength of their lungs and when election and other promises were not flashed around the world with the speed of light.

An obvious question arises: what happens to those in authority who—for the general good—are obliged to take unpopular measures?

As we know, every leader, every executive, every commanding officer often has to do things or issue orders which arouse the anger at least of a minority; on a smaller scale, judges have to sentence criminals and employers have to fire incompetent or dishonest employees. Are they to be penalized by hostile thoughts for doing their duty?

Nature must have made some provision for such situations, if only because, otherwise, the future development of the more promising entities would be needlessly impeded. And we can find a clue to what that provision probably is.

This is that thought-transmission between two people is only possible if there is some kind of sympathy between them. A leader or executive with high motives and intelligence is 'not on the same wave-length' as selfish people too stupid and self-centred to realize that he is acting for the general good. It seems unlikely, therefore, that their vindictive thoughts can harm him. On the other hand a man with entirely selfish or criminal motives is within the same 'band of thought-frequencies'—so to speak—as the angry or vindictive thoughts he arouses by his actions and is therefore vulnerable to them.

It seems likely, too, that the 'reversible reactions' of thought, which we discussed earlier, operate in such cases: a man who is *deliberately* cruel or harsh to others must get back similar reactions from those he has harmed—on the principle that like attracts like.

No doubt the actions and reactions of thought on the entity are far more complex than has been suggested. No doubt, too, many other factors of which we know nothing are involved—Nature is infinitely subtle. But the foregoing may be at least a partial approach to the way in which she applies the brakes on human conduct.

5

To look at the other side of the coin, if we have won the affection or gratitude of others, we may expect their thoughts to follow us and to invigorate our entities, in much the same way that optimistic thoughts benefit our health or mother-love helps infants. And, as affection or gratitude are automatically sympathetic with those who aroused them, there would be no problem about such thoughts reaching and strengthening the entity.

All this suggests that the 'golden rule' which is common to all the great religions, is much more than a beautiful ideal: *it may have a rational and practical basis.*

It would seem rational and practical, too, to try not to flunk the examinations of the University of Earth, however tough and unpleasant they may be. If we can at least scrape through them somehow, we may assume that we shall not have to take them again, somewhere else and in some other form, because Nature's purpose is development, not repetition. Even more important, the more examinations we can pass —the more we can develop the character and stamina of our entities—the better qualified we shall be for pleasanter, more interesting and more exciting experiences in our future existence—just as in this one better degrees win us better jobs.

As far as we can see all Nature's experiments are progressive: the whole trend is towards greater variety. As there is no reason to suppose that her experiment with the human race is any exception to this rule, it is safe to assume that the more the entity develops itself, the greater the scope it will have to use *and enjoy* its freedom. This, perhaps, is the real meaning of Christ's injunction to 'lay up treasures in heaven'.[4] And this, surely, is a more rational, exciting, and appealing prospect than the insipid, semi-effeminate 'heavens' promised by most religions.

<h1 style="text-align:center">6</h1>

Whether we look at the stars and planets in their courses or examine the miraculous processes of life, we see abundant evidence of faultless organization. Only human affairs *seem* to be an exception to the general rule. But we are not justified in saying that they are because we can only see a tiny segment of the curve of human progress and the whole history of the human race to date has taken up only an insignificant fraction of the time that the Universe has been going. Moreover, Nature has given man some freedom—with results which can look like disorganization from our restricted point of view.

But Nature, with all eternity to work with, must see the human experiment in an entirely different perspective. What seems to us disorganization is doubtless a temporary and carefully-organized part of her experiment—we ourselves have to 'disorganize' eggs to make an omelette. It would seem wiser to assume then, with all the evidence of organization around us, that Nature knows what she is doing, even if we don't; and that the human experiment is no exception to the general rule.

A faultless organization cannot tolerate any disorganized

parts. Nor can it ignore the fact that the human donkey, with his measure of freedom, needs either the carrot or the stick: and must make provision for both.

If we think about it for a moment, most of us will find it impossible to believe that the perfect organization of the Universe could tolerate the inefficiencies, uncertainties, delays and mistakes of human legal systems or, for that matter, the ponderous, slow and sometimes uncertain methods by which human organizations hand out rewards or awards of various kinds. It is equally impossible to believe that Nature needs to be bribed or placated—or can be 'fixed' or hoodwinked.

If we cannot believe this kind of thing our only reasonable alternative is to assume that the laws which govern human conduct operate as precisely, impersonally, inevitably and automatically as all other natural laws, such as the law of gravity.

When we see these laws in operation we do not think of Nature as being wrathful or vindictive. If a man falls over a cliff, we do not regard his death as a 'punishment': handed out by a trigger-tempered Nature. We feel that he has automatically suffered the certain consequence of ignoring the natural law of gravity.

Similarly, it would seem that the immortal entity is not 'punished' for its 'sins' but *by* them—by ignoring natural laws.

When we are accustomed to something, it is always hard to imagine anything better. We have become so accustomed to the methods and paraphernalia of human legal systems that it is not easy to realize that Nature—employing the instant and infallible processes of thought—needs neither judges, juries, detectives, courts, beadles, briefs, counsel, writs or policemen. Steeped in ancient traditions, too, inherited from earthy, primitive tribes, we have become accustomed to thinking of angry and vindictive deities, alert to punish and thirsty for bribes or 'sacrifices'. Such ingrained ideas are difficult to shed, even though many find them intellectually indigestible.

Now, however, that modern research into the nature of thought offers a more rational alternative, it is not so hard to shed them and to credit Nature with more efficiency, integrity and good-temper than we had supposed. For surely it is easier to believe that the human entity writes its own 'penalties' and that it builds, in its eternal memory, its own individual 'hell' or 'heaven' out of its own experience and out of the thoughts it has aroused in others.

CHAPTER SEVEN

'What's Past is Prologue'

'...what's past is prologue; what to come, in
yours and my discharge.'
—*The Tempest*

'The Body of
B. Franklin, Printer
(Like the Cover of an Old Book
Its contents torn out
And stript of its Lettering and Gilding)
Lies here, Food for Worms.
But the Work shall not be lost;
For it will, (as he believ'd), appear
Once More
In a new and elegant Edition
Revised and corrected
By the Author
—Benjamin Franklin's own epitaph

1

Where does the eternal entity exist when it is not
imprisoned in a human body? Where does it use its accumulated experience? Where does it enjoy the 'heaven'—or suffer
the 'hell'—it has created for itself, as suggested in the last
Chapter?

There are no certain answers, of course, to these questions.
But what we have found out enables us to make a few
educated guesses.

Since the entity can exist in—and traverse—space, in
theory, at least, it can go anywhere in the Universe. In practice, however, there must be a great variety of conditions—
the 'many mansions' to which Christ referred—and, on the
principle that like attracts like, no doubt the entity 'finds its
own level' and is drawn to places and conditions which are

congenial or to which it is best suited. It seems improbable, for instance, that a scientific genius would spend the next existence under the same conditions as a manual labourer.

As it is non-physical, we would not expect the entity to be affected by extremes of heat and cold; and, without a human body, it will no longer require water or oxygen. If it needs some kind of form or 'body' in which to function, Nature, no doubt, can supply the equivalent of the human L-field but one adapted to building a form of entirely different materials or even fields of energy. (There are references, by the way, in religious and occult writings to a 'body of light.') Probably many kinds of extra-terrestrial L-fields are available to build forms suited to any kind of material or space environment, whether in the heat of Venus or in the cold of the distant planets; for there is no limit to the ingenuity and resource of Nature.

There is at least a good chance, then, that after we die we may be able to do a certain amount of space-exploration on our own, without effort or discomfort, without benefit of rockets or capsules—and at no cost to ourselves or the taxpayer. Many, perhaps, will find this a more appealing prospect than the 'eternal rest' promised by the Churches.

But we have to consider another possibility, which some will find less attractive: if we have not graduated from the University of Earth when we die, we may have to return to this planet for further semesters and courses in human bodies. In other words, we have to consider the possibility of reincarnation. And we must approach it as objectively as possible because this subject is apt to arouse violent emotions.

If we agree that conception—a physical event—cannot *create* two non-physical things, the L-field and the entity, we are left with two choices. Either we must assume that these were mysteriously and specially created at the moment of conception or else that they must have existed *before* the fusion of the sperm and ovum.

To adopt the first choice is to assume that Nature, the supreme organizer, is subservient to human desires—or miscalculations.

Surely it is easier to believe that ready-made L-fields are always available in a common pool—as suggested earlier—

and can start to organize an embryo in the womb as soon as conception has provided the right molecular conditions? In support of this is the fact that all human bodies are similar and their general design has not altered essentially for 100,000 years. If Nature created a fresh L-field for every conception one would expect her to have indulged her zest for variety by making bigger changes in the design over this period.

Entities, on the other hand, are all individual; and all are different—some very different—from each other. If we suppose that they are drawn from some common pool we have to explain how they became different—how, for instance, a Shakespeare or an Einstein developed his individual genius.

An entity—as we have seen—is an experience-gathering organization; and to learn by experience is the reason for its existence. Since all of us are born different, with varied and unequal talents and aptitudes, it seems reasonable to suppose that our entities existed before we were born and acquired different kinds of knowledge and experience in previous existences. Otherwise, we have to explain why, at the moment of conception, they are suddenly created all different, which would violate Nature's normal practice of making changes slowly.

There is no reason to suppose that the entity can exist *only* in a human body or that *all* its existences, before or after its present life on this planet, are spent in the University of Earth —it may well enjoy long sojourns elsewhere. But if it can occupy its present body there seems to be no reason why it should not have occupied others in the past or why it cannot also use others in the future.

To a few in the West and millions in the East this seems to be the only way to explain why all of us are born different: we enter the University of Earth with different credits acquired from past experiences, which qualify us for certain courses, tough or easy, in the present semester.

Whether or not it appeals to us personally, reincarnation has an important bearing not only on the four questions we are trying to answer but also on many of our present problems. For if we are the products of our own past experience, we are personally responsible for the 'grades', with which we started the present semester, and therefore for the 'courses' in this University to which we are assigned.

If this is so, we cannot blame others for our present state and we can also see the apparent unfairness and injustices of human existence in an entirely new light.

2

For this reason, to know where we come from is much more important—as far as the practical problems of this existence are concerned—than to know where we go to after we die. Yet, oddly enough, most Christians ignore their origin and are chiefly interested in their destination—which may account for some of the present problems of Christianity.

True, some Christians who are not enthusiastic about the Theory of Evolution or modern gene theories assume in a vague sort of way that their 'souls' were 'sent by God'. But this does not explain why God 'sent' them all different— still less why the Merciful God of the Christians 'sends souls' destined to live in crippled, diseased or deformed bodies or 'souls' condemned to spend their earth lives in insane asylums.

In the East great thinkers have found *karma* and the doctrine of re-birth the only reasonable and logical way to explain such human misfortunes. In the West, however, most of those who have heard of *karma* are apt arrogantly to dismiss it as superstition partly, no doubt, because they cannot imagine that people who are short of space rockets, automobiles, modern plumbing, or pop-up toasters can know more about some things than they do.

So little, in fact, has *karma* been considered in the West that no word exists for it in English; and the Oxford Universal Dictionary has to define it with the mouthful: 'the sum of a person's actions, in one of his successive states of existence, regarded as determining his fate in the next; hence necessary fate or destiny following as effect from cause.' In simpler terms: our state in our present lives, whether good or bad, is the result of what we have done or learned in previous existences; and what we do in this life, will determine conditions in the future.

There are, of course, many exceptions to the supercilious attitude of the West towards *karma*. According to Dr. Gina Cerminara,[1] the concept of reincarnation has been 'thoroughly accepted' by such distinguished historical figures as Plato, Pythagoras, Virgil, Ovid, Giordano Bruno, Schelling, Leibnitz, Shopenhauer, Fichte, Flammarion, Emerson, Walt Whitman, Carlyle, Edison, Luther Burbank and Henry Ford —to mention a few.

In recent times, no less a person than General George S. Patton, Jr. did not hesitate to express his conviction that he had lived and fought in previous lives on earth. The remarkable motion picture 'Patton' and an excellent book by the General's nephew* show that Patton not only was certain that he had lived before but also could recall details of past lives, battles and places.

Most of the Christian clergy, however, still react to the idea in much the same way as Queen Victoria bridled at an off-colour story.

As a result, discussion of reincarnation today is often frowned on almost as much as discussions of sex, syphilis or birth control used to be; and many sane and serious people who think reincarnation makes sense hesitate to mention it even to intimate friends for fear of being thought irreligious or peculiar. For reincarnation is not only taboo to the Churches but also is sometimes espoused by the type of person with whom solid citizens would not want to be identified.

Though the taboo is breaking down and more and more of the general public are interested in reincarnation—as any bookstore or newsstand shows—Christian leaders, with some distinguished exceptions, still regard a subject of great potential importance as not even fit for discussion.

This is all the more strange because reincarnation is really implicit in Christianity. For Christians believe that Jesus Christ existed, as the Son of God, *before* He incarnated in human form. They believe that His purpose was to induce men to behave like Him; and that it is within their power to do so. But men can hardly do this if they have an entirely different kind of nature and origin. And, if they have, surely

* *Before the Colors Fade* by Fred Ayer, Jr. Boston: Houghton Mifflin Company.

Christ would have mentioned this and would not have expected them to be like Him?

3

By one of the most diverting ironies of history, this strange attitude of most twentieth century divines is partly the result of the ruthless intrigues of an over-sexed, Middle-Eastern courtesan who lived about 1,400 years ago. She was Theodora, daughter of a bear feeder, who became the mistress and then the wife of the Byzantine Emperor Justinian.

At that time many Christians accepted reincarnation as an essential part of Christianity. They followed the teachings of Origen, one of the most brilliant scholars of the early Christian Churches, who, some 250 years earlier, had written in his *De Principiis*: 'Every soul ... comes into this world strengthened by the victories or weakened by the defeats of its previous life. Its place in this world as a vessel appointed to honour or dishonour is determined by its previous merits or demerits. Its work in this world determines its place in the world which is to follow this.'

This philosophy infuriated Theodora who wanted to believe—and wanted the public to believe—that her activities in this world would ensure her an even more prominent position in the next. She expected, in other words, an instant 'heaven' and naturally took a dim view of any suggestions that she might have to earn a 'heaven' by successive incarnations in which to expiate her misdeeds. So she stopped at nothing to purge Christianity of such notions.

It seems likely that she even arranged the murder of two Popes because they opposed her, according to a fascinating study of her tortuous machinations by the novelist and playwright, Noel Langley.[2] And after her death, her husband, Justinian, who also expected an instant 'heaven', drove the last nails into the coffin of reincarnation by convening, in the year 553, the Fifth Ecumenical Church Council which—in modern terms—was carefully 'rigged' to declare that reincarnation was anathema.

No doubt the Emperor and his ecclesiastical stooges ordered the destruction of any embarrassing writings they could lay their hands on, in order to wipe out the last traces of teachings of reincarnation—an easy thing to do before the days of printing. And these writings may well have contained some of the 'pearls' which Christ warned His disciples must not be 'cast before swine'—an approach to security, by the way, which would have raised an epic howl about the public's 'right to know' if there had been any newspapers in those days. But Justinian and his minions did not do a complete job of censorship and there are still a few references in the Bible and Apocrypha which, at least, suggest that reincarnation was accepted as a matter of course.[3]

At first glance, it is hard to understand why, in all this time, the Christian Churches have never questioned the theology of a dissolute Emperor and Empress and an obviously-bogus Council. But there are probably two reasons for this:

For many centuries the authority and dogma of the Churches were rarely challenged, partly because any who dared to do so were likely to receive most painful and un-Christian treatment. More important, the early Christian leaders, struggling to advance the power of the Church, probably found the ideas of Theodora and Justinian politically more effective than the teaching of reincarnation. For to promise an instant 'heaven' or 'hell' gave them more power and authority than to teach the doctrine of reincarnation, which promises not only a second chance but also many chances.

Dogma, once crystallized, is hard to discard or modify, as we can see from the anguished theological discussions of the present time. So we should sympathize with our modern clergy who, through no fault of their own, are trapped in a theological cage fabricated—strangely enough—by the daughter of a feeder of caged bears 1,400 years ago.

4

With this background, the opposition of the Churches to the concept of reincarnation can hardly be regarded as a valid reason for doubting it. Nor need we worry about the prejudices of a nympho Empress and her weak-minded spouse or the political expediencies of the early Churches. But we should consider other reasons why many do not accept reincarnation.

One is the fact that most of us—including this reporter—have not the dimmest conscious recollection of the details of any previous existence. But if our analysis of memory and of the function of the brain-cells was correct, it is easy to see why this is so, even if we have lived before on this planet.

It was suggested that the T-fields of memory have to be 'anchored' to—or localized in—the three-dimensional organization of brain-cells before we can have conscious access to them. As we are born with brand-new brains, memories, if any, of previous existences have no anchorage in the new cells and therefore we cannot be aware of them; and, in any case, we are fully preoccupied with 'recording' the knowledge and experience we need for this existence. This recording process—as Dr. Wilder Penfield's experiments suggest—is the result of *conscious attention* and since, normally, there is nothing to bring past experiences to our attention, we do not record them in our new brains.

As Dr. Penfield has written[4]: 'Only those things to which a man paid attention are preserved in the record or added to the automatic mechanism. The sights and the sounds and the somatic sensations that he ignored are not preserved in any engram form. . . . What a man has ignored leaves no discoverable trace.' This refers, of course, only to memories of our present lifetime.

Sometimes, however, something does happen which seems to bring past memories to consciousness. A visit to some strange place or some startling event can sometimes eject a package of memory from the depths of the entity's 'freezing compartment' and arouse conscious recollection of a past existence. (Some authorities claim that this can also be done by hypnotic regression but this is an experiment the writer has had no desire to try.)

Such cases—more common than is generally realized—sometimes produce recollections which are not only detailed and embarrassing but which can also be confirmed in various ways.

For instance, an Indian Maharaja, of keen intelligence and

complete integrity, once gave this reporter details of a case in his own State, which he and his staff had personally investigated. The sight of her mother laid out for burial evoked memories of a past life in a little girl, who then insisted on visiting her former home and son. The Maharaja and his staff were able to confirm the accuracy of some of the things the little girl remembered—events that had happened *before she was born*.

Another friend of the writer, a successful down-to-earth, Yankee businessman, told him that when as a young man, he was stranded in a strange town in the West, he found that he was familiar with certain features *as they had been many years before* as inquiry confirmed. Some readers may have had similar experiences or know friends who have had them.

In recent years, some outstanding cases have been carefully and scientifically investigated by Dr. Ian Stevenson; and readers who are interested are recommended to read his scholarly book, *Twenty Cases Suggestive of Reincarnation*.[5]

Since most of our memories of our present existence are lost to conscious recall, it is not surprising, apart from the reasons suggested, that most of us cannot remember anything of any previous existences we may have had. This, no doubt, is a good thing. There are enough things in the lives of most of us which we would like to forget; and we have enough to worry about without being burdened with memories of the failures, disasters or disappointments of the past.

On the other hand, though we cannot remember *details* of any previous existence we are certainly born not only with different talents and aptitudes but also with different tastes and preferences. We must surely have acquired these *somewhere* and, although we cannot remember how or where, these things, nonetheless, are a form of memory.

Some people are born with an exceptional talent for some peculiarly human occupation, such as playing the piano or playing baseball, which calls for an unusual control of muscles or eyes. Surely such talents could only have been developed in human bodies in previous lives on this planet, whatever other qualities may have been acquired elsewhere?

We can imagine that mathematicians, artists or writers could have gained their knowledge and skill in some non-human form of existence. But an infant prodigy who can play the violin in the nursery must surely have had violins and human muscles with which to practise.

Many normal children know from their tenderest years exactly what they want to be when they grow up, often long before they can know what the chosen career is really like and sometimes against the advice or wishes of their parents; and they never waiver from that decision. This suggests that some unconscious memory has prompted them.

There are archaeologists who feel an irresistible urge to study some particular set of ruins and who will obsessively devote their lives to one hole in the ground. Surely this suggests some past association?

To those, then, who maintain that reincarnation cannot be true because they cannot remember any past lives, there are two answers. First, there is a lot of suggestive evidence that some people can and do. Second, that they themselves may *unconsciously* 'remember' more than they realize.

5

Apart from this objection, most of the opposition to the idea of reincarnation seems to be more emotional than rational. Many cannot accept it because it is so different from the conventional ideas of 'heaven' and 'hell' in which they have been brought up; and, like Theodora, they find the prospect of an 'instant heaven' more appealing.

Some, too, who go to Church every Sunday and contribute heavily to Church funds do not welcome the idea that this is no guarantee of the comfortable heaven they have been led to expect. And unethical 'robber-baron' types who believe that a substantial donation to some Foundation or Building Fund, followed by a suitable death-bed repentance, will square their accounts with their Maker naturally resent any suggestion that they may have to work off their debts to their victims in future lives.

Some find it hard to accept reincarnation because there are many more people alive on earth today than there were in known ancient times and the earth's population is currently exploding. Where, it is asked, do all these entities come from?

We can only guess; but there are three possibilities, each of which may be part of the explanation. First, it may be that intervals between earth lives are being shortened and that entities who, so far, have only been here at long intervals are now coming back all together. Second, perhaps enrolments in the University are swollen at the present time by entities coming here for the first time. Third, there is some evidence that great civilizations existed before recorded history and the earth, at one time, may have been more densely-populated than we suppose. Those early inhabitants may be crowding back in this age.

Another reason why many dislike the idea of reincarnation is easily understood: after an exhausting and, perhaps, unhappy life on this earth they do not like the prospect of starting another one and prefer the idea of 'eternal rest'—without stopping to reflect that this would soon bore them stiff, like some retired executives.

This natural reaction, however, overlooks three possibilities: reincarnation may not be necessary at all; if it is necessary there may be a long interval before it happens; and, anyway, the next life on earth may be far happier and more successful.

All those who have studied the theory of reincarnation agree that those who have passed all the tests earth-life has to offer them and who have not incurred obligations to others on this planet do not have to incarnate again, unless they want to do so in order to complete some cherished project or to fulfill some ambition. They also agree that reincarnation is not necessarily immediate, that intervals between lives on this planet are often long—frequently hundreds of years; and that, normally, there is always an adequate vacation between semesters at the University of Earth. This supported by such experiences as that of the Yankee businessman mentioned above. He remembered the strange town as it had been *many* years before.

Students of reincarnation also maintain that those who pass the tests and surmount the difficulties of their present lives do not have to repeat the same experience; and that if, for some reason, it is necessary for them to spend another life on earth, it will be an entirely different one, with fresh and greater opportunities for achievement and happiness.

If they are right, the idea of reincarnation need not be depressing even to those who are weary of this life; and to those who get interest and enjoyment out of it, it can be attractive and exciting.

6

Since so many books on reincarnation are now available, there is no need to speculate further on how it works out in practice. Perhaps the most interesting—and convincing—of these are based on the work of the famous American seer, the late Edgar Cayce, because these give actual 'case histories'.[6]

As many people know, Cayce, with a conventional religious upbringing, came to accept the idea of reincarnation most reluctantly and only as the result of his diagnoses of many of his patients. Admittedly, his trance 'readings' are not evidence in the legal sense. But his physical diagnoses were so penetrating and successful that his psychological diagnoses, based on reincarnation, at least deserve serious attention from people with open minds.

Cayce, of course, was unique but, in the light of what we have found, he need not seem mysterious, because we can get at least a rough idea of how he was able to diagnose perfect strangers, perhaps hundreds of miles away. We have a clue in the fact that thought has field properties and can produce effects across space.

It would seem that, when Cayce's conscious mind was temporarily switched-off by sleep or trance, some part of the field of his entity was able to extend its perception across space and to make contact with the entity of the patient. From this it was able to learn the exact physical condition or psychological history of the patient, and by operating the speech mechanisms of Cayce's brain, to dictate a complete and lucid diagnosis to his secretary, while he slept.

It is not generally realized that the ability to diagnose at a distance was not confined to Cayce and that many people in different parts of the world have been—and are—doing it in a different way. They use the same property of the entity to extend its field in space and to make contact with the entity of the patient. But they have to extract the information from the distant entity by laborious techniques of mental 'questions'—on a 'yes' or 'no' basis rather like that of a computer—and with the aid of special instruments. They do not have Cayce's unique ability to present the information obtained directly as a description. On the other hand, they do not need Cayce's remarkable powers; with a little practice about five ordinary people in ten can make diagnoses in this way.

This reporter has investigated this work in different parts of the world over a period of many years. He has had the privilege of knowing personally some of the pioneers, has studied their methods and tried out their instruments himself under experimental conditions. This long investigation has convinced him that they are using a genuine phenomenon of immense potential value to medicine.

Like most of the really important discoveries in medical history, however, this has either been ignored or ridiculed by most of the medical profession. Some doctors and some scientists have not stopped at ridicule and, with various tricks and pressures, have done their utmost to discredit or ruin the pioneers. On one occasion, with the aid of the police, they drove one of them to suicide. And another was ruined financially, defending himself against false charges which had been encouraged by vindictive doctors. In these circumstances, to protect others from possible persecution, the writer cannot give any names of those engaged in this important work.

But that is another story, too long to go into here. It is mentioned merely to make Cayce's work easier to accept by showing that others can do some of the things he did, though in a different and cumbrous way.

Unlike Cayce, however, they cannot get much information about the past lives of a patient. This is because they have to work on a question-and-answer basis and cannot know what questions to ask. To diagnose physical or mental illness they can run through lists of standard questions, to which their instruments will give a 'yes' or 'no' signal; and there are various ways of narrowing down the possible questions. But to attempt to get the story of a patient's past lives would be like trying to programme a computer to write history.

From what we have found, all this need not seem at all 'spooky'. Since the processes of thought are not affected by distance, there is no reason why one entity cannot communicate information to another, if it wishes to do so. As the entity is intimate association with the L-field of the body, we would expect it to be aware of what is really wrong with its own body or brain and to be able to give this information to another entity.

Since, too, the entity retains—in the form of T-fields—'astonishingly detailed' memories of this existence despite the constant 'deaths' of the brain-cells, there is no reason why it should not also retain—in its 'freezing compartment'—detailed memories of previous existences, which it can also communicate to another entity if it wants to.

We can begin to understand, then, a little of the way in which Cayce was able to get information from his distant patients. As he was so often right about their physical ills and helped so many people we should not underestimate his information about their past lives. Certainly, his patients often found that it made sense to them and was helpful in their problems; and occasionally it was possible to confirm some of it from old records.

7

Many questions naturally suggest themselves:

If reincarnation is a fact, how is it organized? Is there some cosmic equivalent of a Dean of Admissions to decide what courses we should take in the University of Earth? Do we have *any* personal choice in the matter? Do we choose our own future parents and the kind of advantages they are able to give us? How do we square our accounts with those we have wronged in a previous life? And so on.

It would be idle to speculate on the answers to such questions, as we have nothing to go on, except our observation of Nature. Everything that we can observe about Nature and the

Universe is marvellously organized in fantastic detail and variety. So it seems safe to assume that, if reincarnation is a fact, it is as perfectly organized as everything else in the Universe; and any natural laws that apply to it must be as precise and inescapable as all the natural laws that we know —and even those of the Internal Revenue Service. For, Nature, as was suggested earlier is not likely to run an important experiment without some controls and some checks and balances, even if we do not know what they are.

As we have a certain amount of free will in this existence, it is reasonable to suppose that we are likely to have some in the next. But it may be of a more restricted kind if, in the next existence, we are able to see more clearly than in this one whether one choice will be worse *for us* than another. There are lots of things in this existence which we *can* do. But, normally, we do not choose to do them if we realize they will be bad for us. Probably, in the next, we shall be able to see consequences more clearly because we should have access to all the knowledge and experience in the 'freezing compartment' of the entity.

With this which, no doubt, will include memories of past mistakes and failures, it is possible that we may freely choose another difficult life on earth because we can see that it will —so to speak—benefit our 'career in eternity'—just as college students freely choose tough courses for the same reason.

In this existence conscience can often restrict free choice as effectively as any dictator. Webster defines conscience as 'Sense of consciousness of the moral goodness or blame-worthiness of one's own conduct, intentions or character, together with a feeling of obligation to do right or be good.' In the next existence, the fully-informed entity may have a much clearer idea of what it ought to do and will freely choose to do it. But here we are getting out of our depth and had better not guess any further.

As we have examined some of the reasons why many reject the concept of reincarnation, it may be useful to summarize some of the factors in its favour in order to help us to form a judgement:

1. Modern discoveries of fields and their properties show that reincarnation is logically and scientifically possible.

2. Reincarnation can offer a reasonable explanation of the inequalities and seeming injustices of human existence, which, otherwise, puzzle and trouble us.

3. It is entirely compatible with Christian belief and many of the early Christians—closer in time to Jesus Christ —accepted it. Its original rejection by the Churches was probably for political reasons and, in 1,400 years, these have never seriously been re-examined.

4. Some of the greatest thinkers of the West and of the East have accepted reincarnation as a fact, as does a large proportion of the world's population today. This great body of opinion should not be disregarded lightly.

5. In our experience, Nature never wastes anything, however much its form may be changed. Modern physics accepts the Law of the Conservation of Mass and of Energy. There is no reason, then, to suppose that human knowledge and experience, painfully acquired, are any exception to the general rule of conservation, even though they are intangible.

6. In all our observations of Nature, development or evolution of any kind takes time and changes are usually made slowly. We must either assume, then, that we had time to develop our different talents and aptitudes in previous existences or else we must explain how we suddenly acquired them and why we are a mysterious exception to the general rule of slow development.

7. Reincarnation is a constructive, virile and hopeful concept, compatible with the widespread human belief in a just God. It can give a new purpose to life. It offers as an incentive cheerfully to endure and surmount the problems of this existence, the prospect of greater opportunities for development, achievement and enjoyment in the future. It also offers us the chance—and the time—to fulfil some mundane ambition or to retrieve some mistake.

Sometimes, it is true, reincarnation has been misinterpreted and has been given the reputation of a passive and fatalistic philosophy. But, as the best students have understood it, it is exactly the opposite—a vigorous philosophy which encourages the individual to stand on his own feet, to assume his own responsibilities and to accept his own mistakes. It is really in keeping with the independent and creative spirit of the pioneers who built the United States and the British Commonwealth.

It does not appeal to the weak-minded, because when we realize that we are products of our individual past we lose some of our pet excuses. We can no longer blame our parents, 'accidents of birth', our 'luck', our friends, our genes or even the government if life for us is not what we would like it to be. For according to the concept of reincarnation our bodies, brains, race, parents, upbringing, tastes, abilities and opportunities are what we have earned in the past and what the entity needs for this stage in its development. We enter the University of Earth with the grade we have earned and are given the courses that are most suitable for us.

If, stripped of our excuses, we feel naked and shivery, we can warm ourselves with the thought that no experience need be wasted and that even the most painful or tragic one can be turned to good account in developing the wisdom, the talents and the fortitude of the entity.

However difficult, too, or depressing or frustrating the present may seem, we can console ourselves with the certainty that an eternal future offers us unlimited time and scope for fresh interest, achievement and enjoyment. Quite literally, in fact, the sky is not the limit.

'What's past is prologue.' But *'what to come in yours and my discharge.'*

In short, our future is up to us.

8

This must be so whether we can accept the idea of reincarnation or whether it annoys us as much as it did Theodora. This does not matter much because we have found reasons why in any case, we must have existed as individuals—*somewhere and in some form*—before we were born.

We know that the entity can exist in space apart from a body and that its purpose is to gather experience. As it can do this in our present existence, despite the constant turn-over of the materials of the brain, we can safely assume that it can go on doing this anywhere without any physical brain at all, either before birth or after death.

Reincarnation can explain why many are born with ready-made assets or liabilities which seem peculiar to life on this planet. But, as we have suggested, other attributes, such as special talents for music, mathematics or art, might well have been developed in a non-physical existence.

If students of reincarnation are right in believing that there are often long intervals between incarnations—some believe that intervals of 200 years are common—it seems un-likely that the entity spends them in complete idleness because nothing in Nature—or human nature—is static. So, in a non-physical existence, the entity can doubtless acquire various kinds of knowledge and experience and can build its own future, good or bad.

In fact, an extra-terrestrial existence may offer far greater opportunities than this one for interesting experience and keener enjoyment—and also for more painful 'penalties'—because the processes of thought are likely to work more swiftly and surely when the entity is free of the restrictions of matter.

Since Nature gives the individual free will in this life and also subjects him to various tests, there can be no doubt that she does the same in other forms of existence. In those as in this the individual can progress or slip back; he can profit by his opportunities or suffer the consequences of flunking his exams. The choice and the responsibility are his alone.

When the time comes for him to be born in a human body, his use—or misuse—of his previous existence will determine the conditions under which he enters the University of Earth and the courses he must take.

We cannot escape the fact that we are all born different. Previous experience—whether in non-physical forms or human bodies or both—is a simple and logical explanation of this.

And it is an explanation which agrees with our ideas of fairness and justice, which—when we come to think of it—we could not possess at all if Nature did not have them also.

CHAPTER EIGHT

The Science of the Future?

'Today there is a wide measure of agreement
. . . that the stream of knowledge is heading
towards a non-mechanical reality; the universe
begins to look more like a great thought than a
great machine. Mind no longer appears as an
accidental intruder into the realm of matter; we
are beginning to suspect that we ought rather to
hail it as the creator and governor of the realm
of matter. . . .'[1]

—Sir James Jeans

1

So far, the term 'Nature' has been used to describe the
creative, organizing force behind life, because this word is
acceptable to most people who realize that there must be
such a force, however they may visualize it. It will not appeal,
of course, to those who do not think there can be any such
thing and that the Universe is an accident. But we can leave
them to flounder in their fantasies.

Some may argue that 'Nature' and 'God' mean the same
thing, which is really a question of definition. But the word
'God' has been avoided in the preceding chapters because
'God' means different things to different people. Even those
who claim to have access to a 'hot wire' to 'God' differ so much
in their interpretations of His wishes and intentions that the
rest of us are tempted to think that somehow they must have
got on a multi-party-line.

So it has seemed simpler, less pretentious and less confusing
to use the word 'Nature'. But, whatever word we use for the
organizing power behind our existence, it is worthwhile to
try to find out a little more about it, because we are a pro-

118

duct of it and, by knowing more about it, can perhaps learn more about ourselves.

Perhaps we should now use the term 'Ultimate Reality' because what we are trying to find is the original, under-lying cause of everything that exists, including ourselves. In doing so, we can cheerfully steer clear of the reefs of theology and mysticism because modern physics has given us another glimpse of the obvious—some clues which were not available before the beginning of this century.

It is now known that all matter is composed of the basic elements in different proportions and arrangements. It is also known that the elements themselves are composed of similar sub-atomic particles in different numbers and arrange-ments. The differences, therefore, between one kind of matter and another or between one element and another lies in the *arrangement—or organization in space—of common, basic components.*

Physics has also shown that the difference between one form of electromagnetic energy and another—for example, between light-waves and radio-waves—is merely one of fre-quency or the number of wave-cycles per second. In other words, the difference between light-waves and radio-waves or between blue light and red is merely one of *organization in time.*

It is also known that the components of atoms sometimes behave like particles and sometimes like waves and many physicists feel that 'wave-mechanics' is the best way to explain their behaviour.

Nuclear physics, too, has demonstrated that matter can sometimes be converted into energy and energy into matter; an organization in space can sometimes be changed into an organization in time—and *vice versa.*

These facts show that the identity—or 'reality'—of every-thing in the Universe depends on something intangible—an *organization* in time or in space or in both. Or, to put it another way, *organization* is the basic, common 'ingredient' of everything.

It is unfortunate that there is no better word for this because 'organizer' and 'organization' have been debased by modern usage. 'Organizer' suggests an agitator stirring up trouble, a management consultant fouling up a business or a dominating female running some improbable charity. And 'organization' is generally used to describe the often-chaotic results of such endeavours.

Webster, however, defines 'to organize' as 'to give an organic structure to' and 'organization' as 'state or manner of being organized; organic structure'. So there is no more suitable word than organization to describe the basic ingredient of everything—from sunshine to rocks, from atoms to living forms.

In all our experience, however, any kind of organization is the product of some intelligence or mind. There can be no organization of any sort—whether it be the plans for a building, the circuitry of a computer or the arrangement of a dinner-table—without the *previous thought* of some mind.

So we can take things one step further and say that the *Ultimate* Reality—the original, essential cause and component of everything—is *Mind or Thought*.

2

Though we have reached this conclusion by a modern route we cannot flatter ourselves that we have found anything new. It has been obvious to some, without benefit of modern physics, for many centuries. For instance, the Vaibhashikas, an early sect of Indian Buddhists, asserted about two thousand years ago 'that atoms exist; that each of them, independently of another, hath space in which to whirl; and that it is due to mind's activity that they have coherence.'[2]

Among the Greek philosophers, Plato and Anaxagoras realized that organization and mind are the basis of everything. Anaxagoras wrote[3] '... mind (*nous*) is infinite and self-powerful and mixed with nothing but it exists alone itself by itself.... And whatever things were to be, and whatever things were, as many as are now, and whatever things shall be, all these mind arranged in order.... Nothing is absolutely separated nor distinct, one thing from another, except mind. All mind is of like character, both the greater and the smaller.'

In this century, some great thinkers and scientists, like

Sir James Jeans, have pictured the Universe as *'consisting'* of the pure thought of a mathematical thinker.[4]

In concluding, then, that Mind or Thought is the Ultimate Reality we find ourselves in respectable company. And we can observe with amusement those who still confuse mind with the physical brain and who imagine thinking to be a purely electro-chemical process. They do not realize that mind or thought is a force in its own right, which can exist and function apart from brains or matter. For all their modern educations and impressive degrees, they are not as smart as the ancient Vaibhashikas or Anaxagoras.

3

There cannot be different kinds of Ultimate Reality because, if there were, nothing could be called 'ultimate'—which Webster defines as 'incapable of further analysis, division or separation; elemental'. The Ultimate Reality which we can also call the Universal Mind, since it consists of Mind, cannot be graded like beef; as Anaxagoras put it, 'all mind is of like character, both the greater and the smaller'.

As 'Ultimate Reality' and 'Universal Mind' are ponderous terms, it will be simpler from now on to use the word 'Essence' to embrace them both. Webster defines 'essence' as 'that in being which underlies all outward manifestations and is permanent and unchangeable; substance'. This seems the best word we can find to describe the mind and organization which are the basis of everything.

We have only to look around to see that the Essence has an infinity of *manifestations,* from stars to seedlings; It is like a great diamond with a myriad facets. But it is all one diamond, of the same flawless quality right through. *And one of its countless facets, or manifestations, is Man.*

Although the human race and each individual entity are probably among the least lustrous facets of the diamond, with, at present, some surface imperfections, they are, none the less, manifestations of the Essence. As such, they must possess Its quality of *permanence* and must play some part, however insignificant, in the Ultimate Purpose.

Since the individual entity is a minute part of the Essence

we would expect it to function on similar lines; and *we have found that it does,* which is significant.

The Essence organizes and controls the matter and energy of the Universe by means of fields. It uses gravitational fields, magnetic and electromagnetic fields, the minute but intensely-powerful fields within the atom and probably many other kinds of field we have yet to discover.* Fields are among the 'tools' by which the Essence, which is pure Mind, manipulates various forms of energy and gross matter. Or, to put it another way, fields are the 'intermediaries' between mind and matter.

Similarly, the intermediary between the human entity—a field of mind—and its physical form is the L-field which organizes and controls the matter and energy of the human body. Normally, it is true, the L-field does this without supervision but sometimes the entity can and does over-ride it as we have seen. Thus the entity, of the same nature as the Essence, can use the same kind of 'tool' as the Essence, in a limited way, to manipulate matter and energy.

Outside his own body man has much greater control over fields and makes extensive use of them, though he cannot do this directly with his mind but has to use instruments and machines. The vast electrical and electronic industries, for instance, are evidence of his practical success in using fields.

As a sub-microscopic manifestation of the universal Essence, the human individual's powers, of course, are utterly insignificant by comparison. But, from our point of view, all that matters is that the individuality has the same *nature* as the Essence. This, surely, means that it cannot be annihilated but *must last as long as the Essence.* As nothing is static, however, we would expect it to change and evolve through eternity.

Here again a modern road has brought us to something which has long been known. Two thousand years ago, for instance, Jesus Christ stated all this simply and poetically when He taught that we are 'children of God' and that 'the kingdom of God is within you' (Luke XVII: 21). And can

---

* This reporter, in fact, has been shown in confidence *instrumental* evidence of the existence of fields of a kind unsuspected by physicists. But this research is not yet sufficiently advanced to be published.

we imagine any better way in which He could have explained these things to the people of those days who knew nothing of fields or physics?

If there are any bounds to the powers of the Essence, we certainly do not know what they are. So we can set no limits to the *potential* of any manifestations of the Essence, including the human entity. Whatever the present limitations of the entity may be, then, we have no reason to suppose that there are any restrictions on its scope in the eternity ahead.

If there are not, our future existences need no longer seem to be a dismal anaesthesia of 'eternal rest'. Far from it: they promise to be as interesting and exciting as we care to make them if we take full advantage of our potential and of the unlimited time in which to develop it.

4

At first sight this idea of an Essence of pure Mind may seem dreary and inhuman especially to those who believe in a Personal God or a Loving Father. It may seem to substitute a chilly, impersonal super-egghead for a warm and friendly father-image. But a little reflection will show that it need not alter anyone's personal concept of God.

As we are all manifestations or parts of the Essence, our imaginations must be a reflection of the infinite imagination of the Essence because we could not have got them from anywhere else. Our mental pictures of God, then, must be insignificant by-products—so to speak—of the imagination of the Essence though, no doubt they are not only restricted by our own limitations but also are distorted by our experience of life on this planet.

Allowing for such defects, it seems fair to say that any personal pictures of God which we may hold in our minds are valid *for us* because the infinite imagination of the Essence must embrace all that man can possibly imagine and countless other things which he cannot begin to visualize.

Sir James Jeans' picture of God, then, as the Supreme Mathematician is as legitimate and justified as the Christian concept of an all-wise Father of infinite love and mercy because the Essence is both—and an infinite number of other things besides. In choosing our personal picture of God, in fact, our choice seems unlimited; and, whatever picture we form in our minds, it is probably no more accurate or inaccurate than the next man's. For the human imagination, at best, can only visualize the crudest pictures of a few of the numberless manifestations of the Essence.

This should make us completely tolerant of the ideas of others about God—however odd they may seem to us—and also of their religious observances because these partly derive from their pictures of God.

There may be one exception to our unlimited choice of pictures: are we justified in visualizing a vindictive or bad-tempered God? The Old Testament idea of an angry and jealous deity, clamouring for 'sacrifices', does not seem compatible with the Essence, especially if we credit It with a sense of humour. Moreover, the Essence gave us a measure of freewill and must surely have foreseen some of the consequences.

It is hard to believe, too, that the Essence—which conceived and controls the intricate and superbly-balanced organization of the Universe—can have the low boiling-point attributed to God by some of the Old Testament characters and by the hell-fire evangelists. Knowing the dangers of driving an automobile when angry we can well imagine what might happen if the Essence ran the Universe in a rage. And surely It cannot be *emotionally* concerned with the 'sins' or 'sacrifices' of Its own creations?

Since we—manifestations of the Essence—can get angry, it might be argued that the Essence Itself must be able to lose Its temper. This, however, seems wildly improbable. Perhaps the answer to this argument is that anger and a desire for revenge are purely human distortions of—or over-reaction to—the sense of fairness and justice which we derive from the Essence. But it would be best to leave this problem to the theologians because science offers no clues to its solution.

Science, however, can suggest an answer to another question about God which some ask themselves: Is it possible to believe that the Creator of an unimaginably vast Universe can take a personal interest in insignificant humans living on just one planet of one of the many millions of stars?

Now that astronomy has shown the immensity of the Universe and the numbers of stars and galaxies that it contains, few can believe that man is the centre of creation—either physically or metaphorically—as was assumed in the days before telescopes. And if man is not the kingpin of the Universe can he expect special individual attention from its Creator?

Physics and biology offer a clue to the solution of this problem. They have shown that inanimate matter, living forms and, in fact, the Universe itself are constructed of standard units or, in engineering parlance, of 'sub-assemblies' —particles, atoms, molecules, cells, organs, planets, stars and galaxies. If we agree that all these things are manifestations of the Essence, which is Mind, it follows that the Essence manifests by what we might call 'units of mind'.

These units range from the infinitely-small, which manifest as particles or atoms, to the gigantic which embrace and organize the billions of smaller units that go to make up a planet, a star or a whole galaxy. Though all these units are lesser or greater parts of larger organizations, they are discrete and have an independent existence of their own; and sometimes they can be exchanged for similar units.

Surely this shows that the creative and organizing powers of the Essence are, so to speak, decentralized? We would expect this because, in our experience, decentralization is one secret of good organization. And this is confirmed by the fact that the Essence has given us free will. By doing so, It has, in effect, decentralized an infinitesimal fragment of Its own creative power and given us the responsibility for using it.

Unless we are so conceited as to think that man is the highest manifestation of the Essence—which is no compliment to It—we must admit that the Universe probably contains far higher intelligences. If the Essence delegates some small powers to man, we would expect It to delegate far greater powers to higher intelligences—to more advanced beings in other states of existence. And some of these may well have overall responsibility for the development of—say —the planet Earth and its inhabitants while others, even more advanced, may have responsibility for our whole solar system. And so on.

As in any good organization we would expect these 'Viceroys of the Essence'—to coin a term—to have many deputies and assistants, to whom they can delegate different tasks and lesser responsibilities. The poet-philosopher, Douglas Fawcett, gave such beings the title of 'Imaginals' and pictured them as having specific responsibilities for the creative development of the various living forms on this planet—from man to mice, from trees to flowers.

If the human entity can use a physical body, there seems to be no reason why these Viceroys and their Deputies should not also assume human form, if they wish to do so in order to guide and assist human development. If, or when, they do we may expect a Moses, a Zoroaster, a Buddha, a Mohammed or a Jesus Christ, all of whom had a profound influence on the human race.

Some may find it easier to believe that a Viceroy of Earth or one of his Deputies can take an interest in their personal problems than to imagine that the Creator of the entire Universe is always available to listen to their prayers. And this more modest belief need not diminish their confidence in prayer because the Viceroy and his Deputies must have all the power, interest, compassion, love and humour that man can possibly need.

A possibility—worth mentioning in passing—has been suggested by Sir Oliver Lodge[5] and others. This is that the entity which occupies a human body is only a part of a larger 'Subliminal Self' which remains in a non-physical existence but which is in constant touch, by thought, with its incarnated portion. If this is so, it may be through the Subliminal Self that the entity can get help and guidance; and at least we would expect it to get personal attention from its own Subliminal Self. If this happens, it may explain how people can unexpectedly rise to an occasion and do things of which they did not think themselves capable; and may, perhaps, be the basis of the old belief in 'Guardian Angels'.

If our Subliminal Selves exist they are the most likely beings to have the time and the incentive to take an interest in our trivial personal affairs. But if Angels exist, they must be more important than our Subliminal Selves and one would expect them to have better things to do than, say, to supervise our driving on the New Jersey Turnpike.

5

This century has produced some vast, world-wide organizations, both for business and for defence. These demand the amazingly-rapid and efficient communications systems of today and, in fact, could not function without them. Despite their efficiency, however, and despite many built-in safeguards these organizations are not infallible, as we know: some minor human error or some detail overlooked can have serious consequences.

These facts of modern life can show us something about the organization of the Universe and the powers of the Essence:

As an organization, the Universe is not only inconceivably immense and complex but also fantastically dynamic. Everything in it, from particles to galaxies, is in a constant state of motion and change. It is not—as some still seem to think—a machine which can run on its own because machines do not change their own components as the Universe does. Stars explode and cool off, radiation varies, comets and meteorites race through space, magnetic fields and climates change, different forms of life appear and disappear. And, to make things more difficult we—and probably other beings elsewhere—have been given some free will and the power to disrupt the organization. In short, the Universe is an organizer's nightmare.

Yet it has been running smoothly for many millions of years and, despite all the changes, the balance of Nature is maintained. Our experience of human organization suggests that this would not have been possible without faultless instantaneous 'telecommunications' within the system—without an omniscient awareness of every detail and event. Otherwise there would have been chaos long ago.

Since relatively-simple human organizations can be damaged by minor errors or neglected details we can assume that the intricate, interdependent organization of the Universe cannot tolerate the smallest piece of *unexpected* grit in the machine. The organization cannot permit any accidents, even if it sometimes seems to us that it does. As someone put it: 'Man's accidents are God's purposes.'

As the Essence is pure Mind and the Universe the product of Its thoughts, Its awareness of events in any part of the Universe must be by means of what we can picture as a 'radar of thought'. This must function instantaneously because we can hardly imagine that the Essence can be kept waiting for information, even for a small fraction of a microsecond.

So vast a Universe, in which everything moves at enormous speeds could not operate if the thoughts of its Organizer were weakened by distance or subject to any delay in transmission —the Universe cannot be measured in 'thought-years'. This need not surprise us because speed is a property of time and distance a property of space. As both time and space are products of the Mind of the Essence we would expect thought to be entirely independent of them.

Thoughts generated by human minds must have properties similar to those of the Essence because human minds are particles of the Essence. When human thoughts are transmitted, therefore, they must use some channel—so to speak— of the telecommunications of the Universe. So it is not surprising that nobody—as far as the writer knows—has ever found that human thought-transmission is either weakened by distance or restricted to the speed of light, which physicists assume to be the ultimate speed of the Universe. Thought is faster—it is instantaneous.

Research into the phenomenon of precognition shows that human thoughts can also be independent of time. Though this is not recognized—and often ridiculed—by the Scientific Establishment history provides abundant evidence for any who care to look for it that some people are able to foretell events before they happen. There have been seers in every age; this reporter, for instance, had a friend—now dead —who told him of something not only nine months in the future but also, at the time she described it, a closely-guarded secret of the British Government of which neither she nor this reporter could have had the slightest suspicion.

From our point of view, the telecommunications of the

Universe have more than an academic interest because they show that our thoughts—under the right conditions—can reach others at any distance instantaneously. In the next existence, therefore, we should be able to contact relatives and friends who have reached it before us without difficulty, delay or recourse to some cosmic Western Union.

This instant awareness of the omniscient Essence of every event and detail was clearly described by Jesus Christ when He said: 'Are not two sparrows sold for a farthing? And one of them shall not fall on the ground without your father. But the very hairs of your head are all numbered.' (Matt. X: 29, 30.)

He also made it clear that the Universe is meticulously organized for some Ultimate Purpose when He said: 'Till heaven and earth pass, one jot or one tittle shall in no wise pass from the law till all be fulfilled.' (Matt. V: 18.)

As mentioned earlier, Einstein is reported to have been searching for a 'unified field' to embrace all the other fields known to physics. There may be such a field which one day, perhaps, another great genius will discover and interpret mathematically.

Meanwhile, we can see that, in the *ultimate* sense, *the 'unified field' is the Essence*, because every field in the Universe is a manifestation of the Essence, always in Its awareness and always under Its control.

Whether this 'unified field' of Mind can ever be explained in terms of human mathematics is doubtful because it is a manifestation of the Supreme Mathematician—the source of all mathematics and the origin of everything in the Universe, including those precise mathematical laws to which the physical Universe is subject. No wonder, then, that Sir James Jeans suggested that the Universe consists of the thought of a mathematical thinker.

6

Though all this is intangible, it is important because, paradoxically, this materialistic, technological civilization is increasingly harassed by intangible problems. Whether we like it or not, we are being hustled into the Era of Intangibles.

Physicists, perhaps, started the process by discovering that something we thought we could be sure of—solid matter—is not solid. They found that the particles of which it is composed sometimes behave more like waves than particles; and that matter can sometimes be converted into waves of energy. But they are unable to answer the question: 'Waves in *what*?' Some, in fact, think this a tactless question and that there is no need for the waves to be in anything—and one can hardly get more intangible than that.

Higher mathematics seems to be getting so much higher that even its favourite intangible, the square root of minus one, look positively earthy by comparison with modern concepts.

As we have seen, 'this too too solid flesh' of our bodies is not really solid but always changing and is controlled by electromagnetic fields which nobody can see or touch.

Inspection of any bookstore reveals a growing public awareness of the reality of another intangible, extra-sensory-perception, in various forms, which stimulates the blood-pressure—though not, unfortunately, the imagination—of the scientific hierarchy.

Then, since this century began, we have suffered the disastrous consequences of two intangibles—Germany's idea of a right to rule the world and Communism's idea of a mission to do the same thing. The former was suppressed—temporarily at least— by two World Wars at an untold cost of blood, misery and treasure. The Communist idea has already cost the world some 20,000,000 lives and incalculable misery and wealth; and still confronts us.

Far-sighted military leaders agree with Abraham Lincoln that 'you cannot shoot an idea'; and some have privately admitted to this reporter that the Idea of Communism can finally be defeated *only* by a better idea. It was they, in fact, who originally encouraged the writer to pursue the present investigation, especially as nobody else seemed to be trying to tackle the problem.

World-wide student unrest—as noted in the first chapter—is partly inspired by a search for a new purpose in life. For lack of this intangible, they seize buildings, wreck offices and scream obscenities at the faculty.

Our growing crime-waves, our all-too-numerous retarded children, and our bulging mental hospitals are partly the result of a lack of other intangibles, parental affection and parental strength of mind. Most people now realize that unwanted children, or children of broken homes, are likely to have emotional problems and to get into trouble. Few realize, however, that they may have serious physical problems as well.

One of the country's foremost paediatricians has shown this reporter horrifying evidence of how 'spiritual deprivation' can stunt or damage the *physical* development of children, quite apart from any emotional effects it may have. Experienced maternity nurses, too, have assured him that they can usually tell from physical signs in the first hours of its life whether a baby is wanted or unwanted. Nobody can estimate, therefore, how much of the present load of physical ailments on our over-taxed hospitals and health services is basically due to the absence of that priceless intangible, parental love.

In recent years we have realized the great problems of pollution and the destruction of natural resources, which are the result of intangibles—selfishness or lack of imagination.

Other examples could be cited to show the importance of intangibles in this century. But these should be sufficient to indicate that this materialistic age is being heavily penalized and taxed for its neglect of intangibles. It follows that a deeper study of intangibles is as pressing as it is practical; and that this study demands as much knowledge as we can muster of the basic and most important intangible, Mind.

At a recent meeting of the American Association for the Advancement of Science some members reportedly asked where science is going. The answer to this seems to be that it is unlikely to go anywhere useful or to do much more than tread water for the rest of this century unless it pays more attention to the underlying cause of everything.

Mind *should* be the important science of the future. Whether it *will* be is problematical because, at present, an impeccable orthodoxy is the secret of successful 'grantsmanship'.

In a few years or decades, however, those who finance grants

131

to science may realize that human problems are more important than technical ones. It may dawn on them that the exploration of space, for instance, is limited by the endurance of astronauts and taxpayers but that the exploration of mind, in all its manifestations, is unbounded—and far less expensive.

When that happens thought will be recognized as a force in its own right and will become a respectable subject for research. Ideas developed by research and backed by the prestige of science will catalyze new attitudes of mind, which will help to resolve many problems. Science as a whole will outgrow its cocksure, materialistic attitudes and understand that mind is the basis of everything and that fields, known and yet to be discovered, are the tools with which it sculptures matter and wields energy. Medicine and biology will appreciate the importance of life-fields and thought fields in the diagnosis and treatment of physical and mental illness; and there will be better and cheaper medicine.

But our great-grandchildren will wonder—with incredulous amusement—why twentieth-century science, with all its brilliant achievements, took so long to rediscover what the Vaibhashikas and the ancient philosophers knew thousands of years ago.

7

Many people today believe that Science is 'ahead of religion', that religion is 'out of date'. Some even say that 'God is dead'. But, if the conclusions reached in the foregoing pages are valid, the fact is that Science is at last catching up with religion and offering some experimental support for what faith has known for centuries. And in the sense that religion realizes that God—or what we have termed the Essence—is the basis of everything and the Ultimate Reality, religion can claim to be way ahead of Science.

Modern research, of course, offers no support for dogma or fringe-beliefs but, as we have seen, it can not only support the *essential* beliefs of the great religions but also can explain them in a new way.

Religion teaches, for instance, that man has an immortal

'soul' independent of his perishable body, but cannot explain what a 'soul' really is. Modern research, however, offers a new and rational explanation:

It has established that memory—the essence of the human personality—survives the constant changes of the material of the brain and must therefore be independent of it. The fact that it is not affected by the perpetual dissolution of its instrument, the brain, is an indication that it can survive the final dissolution of the body.

Research has also shown that the human body is built, maintained and repaired by an electromagnetic field, which can be influenced and over-ridden by another kind of field, the human mind. The former can be measured with volt-meters; and although the latter cannot be measured with instruments, some of its *effects* can be. We have seen that the state of the mind can produce measurable electrical changes in the field.

Mind, like memory, must be a manifestation of what religions refer to as 'soul' or 'spirit'—it cannot be a product of the body (though it may be influenced by it) because mind and memory are permanent and the body always changing. The fact, then, that mind can produce measurable and repeatable electrical changes—Science's criterion of a valid phenomenon—is evidence that mind and its source, the 'soul' are realities, independent of the body.

There is abundant evidence—admittedly not yet recognized by Science—that thought or mind can behave like a field, within the accepted definition of a field. Since fields can exist in—and traverse—space without any material manifestation, the fields of mind and memory, the essence of the 'soul', can exist and travel apart from human bodies.

Physicists tell us that the only way to destroy a field is to remove its source. We have just discussed the reasons for supposing that the human entity is a particle of the Ultimate Reality or Essence. As it is clearly impossible to destroy the Essence we may safely assume that all of Its manifestations, however insignificant, are part of Its purpose and equally durable. This is compatible with Christ's promise of eternal life for the 'children of God'.

Most religions emphasize the worth and importance of the

individual. We have deduced this from modern knowledge.

All religions teach the 'Golden Rule' and we have seen why it has a rational and practical basis.

Most religions promise—not too convincingly—rewards or punishments in the next life. Our examination of the properties and effects of thought shows how we build our own 'heavens' or 'hells' though these, admittedly, do not include the 'judgement day' envisaged by some religions.

Admittedly, too, orthodox Christianity does not believe that the human entity exists before it is born, even though it concedes a previous existence to its Founder. We have found good reasons for thinking that we must exist before we were born and that reincarnation is theoretically possible—if not probable—but not necessarily inevitable. Neither previous existence nor reincarnation conflict with any teachings of the Founder. In fact, as we have seen, it is probable that reincarnation was accepted without question by the more intellectual of the early Christians.

We rarely pause to reflect that most of the dogma of organized religion is purely man-made and often has little justification in the teachings of the Founder. When we do realize this, we can see that the 'ecumenical' conferences of the present time have little relation to reality and little chance of more than a limited success.

Here is a strange situation: While earnest leaders of the Churches solemnly—and sometimes inflexibly—debate fine points of ancient doctrine many of their members, especially of the younger generation, seek urgently and vainly for some new understanding of reality and of the purpose of life, as Dr. Tillich has observed. Meanwhile, quite unbeknownst to the leaders of the Churches, science has unwittingly offered them new support for their essential beliefs and some highest common factors on which reasonable adherents of many different faiths can agree.

Modern researches into the properties of thought can also help religion. They can offer religion new insights into the nature of prayer, clues to more effective 'faith-healing' and even an entirely new reason for going to church—the fact that churches can serve to generate powerful fields of helpful and creative thought.

Though many of the prayers of a congregation may be muddled, selfish or depressing and though some of their thoughts are doubtless un-Christian, on balance the thoughts of most congregations are probably helpful, especially if they are stimulated by good music and focused by impressive ritual. That is why a casual visitor to a church may feel refreshed and inspired even if the service is in a language which he does not understand. And since thoughts can localize themselves in bricks and mortar, a visitor can sometimes get a 'lift' from an empty church, especially if it has been used for many years.

8

Religion is primarily concerned with human minds and attitudes and with man's relationship to his Creator. For this reason it is more closely associated with the Ultimate Reality than science and should be more important. In theory, at least, religion should be the Dominant Science with all the other branches of science auxiliary and complementary. This, of course, would be something broader, more comprehensive and more universal than modern 'Christian Science' because a Dominant Science would draw its strength from every branch of knowledge and could appeal to adherents of many different faiths both in the East and the West.

Before modern science reduced the authority and influence of religion, it was the dominant—and only science—in many civilizations; the priests and the scientists were the same. Now that science offers some support for man's beliefs, religion not only has the opportunity to regain its former influence but also to extend it because it can use the universal language of science. With a scientific appeal and with modern communications, it could greatly enhance its prestige and augment its congregations.

That, of course, is purely theoretical. In practice, the shackles of inflexible dogma and outworn tradition will probably make it impossible for religion to seize the ball and carry it.

Despite its strait-jackets, however, religion can do a lot. As it cannot lick Science it can join it and make use of it without losing face. It can adapt its findings to interpret its teachings to a scientific age. It can avail itself of all the latest studies of mind and thought and bend them to its task of alleviating human problems and miseries.

Clergy and candidates for Holy Orders, for instance, could usefully spend more time studying the effects of mind on the body than the doctrinal theories of long-dead theologians. They could learn, too, something about hypnotism and its potential effect because religion—especially in the form of 'revivals'—often induces a kind of auto-hypnosis; and the more that the clergy understand the possibilities and limitations of hypnotism, the better. They should also be fully informed of the physical and mental effects of the 'spiritual deprivation' of unwanted children and warn their congregations accordingly.

Christian clergy, especially, should know as much as possible about modern research into thought so that they can more effectively carry out the often-forgotten injunction of the Founder to 'heal the sick'—whether their ills be mental or physical.

In short religion should cease to think of modern knowledge as an enemy and should welcome it as an ally.

Whether or not it will do so, whether religion will ever become the Dominant Science, these are questions to which the answers lie hidden in the mists of the future.

CHAPTER NINE

New Perspectives

Just as doctors' orders mean such and such
treatment as specific for such and such complaint,
so every individual has circumstances ordered for
him specifically in the way of destiny. . . .

Nothing happens to a man that nature has not
made him for.

—Marcus Aurelius

1

Whatever science or religion may do or think there is
nothing to stop us from making immediate use of anything
that we have found which may help to solve our personal
problems, to illuminate our uncertainties or to relieve our
anxieties.

We have assembled a mosaic of facts and phenomena which
anyone can check for himself, if he cares to take the time
and trouble. We have looked at this mosaic in the light of
ordinary common sense and have tried to interpret its meaning. If our conclusions seem valid to us we are fully entitled
to accept them and to act on them without advice or assist-
ance from priests, professors or pundits. For most of them
know nothing about the things we have considered and a
Ph.D. has no monopoly of common sense. In fact the world's
most extensive and expensive educational system offers no
sheepskins for this subject.

As far as the writer knows, the trail we have blazed is a new
one, even though it has led us to some conclusions which are
as old as time. There are no experts on new trails; and the
reader who has followed it is as qualified as anyone to judge
its usefulness. Indeed his judgement is likely to be more
reliable than one made with a closed mind—blinkers of
prejudice are a handicap in blazing new trails.

As stated in the first chapter, this investigation is a 'do-it-yourself' project which the reader can adapt to his own personal problems. He will be able, too, to widen and improve the trail we have followed and to smooth out the rough spots.

We have neither expected nor found complete and perfect answers to all the questions we have raised. In reality, too, things are undoubtedly far more complicated than they seem from such facts we have been able to assemble; the human entity, for instance, is probably far more complex and composed of more fields than has been suggested. But half a loaf is better than no bread.

In an age in which many make a profession of gobbledegook and obscurity over-simplification has its uses, as long as we realize that it is over-simplification. It can at least clear our minds and serve as a foundation for more elaborate structures.

2

If the conclusions we have reached make sense to us, there are various ways in which they can be immediately helpful because they can give us new perspectives on life:

If we can convince ourselves that our present lives are merely temporary interludes in an eternal existence, we need not take such a dim view of their sorrows, problems or frustrations. Most things are easier to take if we *know* they are only temporary.

Many of us have had to wrestle with dreary, difficult or dangerous problems away from home and under unpleasant living conditions. If—as often happens—there is no compensating excitement or interest, we cannot enjoy such assignments but they do not 'get us down' because we know they are only temporary. The certainty that 'this, too, will pass' can give us a better lift than any pep-pill or martini.

For most of us the 'American Dream' must always remain largely a dream. In theory there is nothing to stop us from achieving all our ambitions or from attaining the highest offices and distinctions. In practice, however, our own limitations and the competition of others better qualified are likely to limit our achievements in one lifetime. But this need neither disappoint nor frustrate us if we realize that this lifetime is merely one episode in an *active* existence, with unlimited time for achievement. We can accept—and eventually realize—the 'Cosmic Dream' of infinite scope in an eternal future.

This certainty can also give us a new perspective on death, as we have already noted. For we have deduced that the entity exists to gather experience and there is no reason to suppose that it abandons the purpose of its existence just because it no longer has a physical form.

This makes death look interesting and exciting: 'To die,' as Peter Pan said, 'will be an awfully big adventure.' Or, as Theodore Roosevelt put it: 'Life and death are part of the same great adventure.' Unless we have blundered badly in this life or have 'flunked out' we can look forward to death partly as a vacation and partly as a transfer to a more interesting University.

It is natural, of course, to fear the *process* of dying, sometimes painful or needlessly prolonged by well-meaning doctors. Even if it is not painful or lingering death is usually an emotional strain on relatives—and often a financial one; and it is always inconvenient and distressing to those close to us. It is natural, too, to dread the idea of parting from family or friends and to be reluctant to leave some project unfinished. *But there is no need to fear the next existence itself*, still less to believe the gloomy pictures painted by some Churches and embellished by the undertaking industry.

On the contrary we can look on death as a fascinating voyage and—in most cases, at least—are justified in feeling rather envious of friends who make the trip before we do. For them we should hold a cheerful *bon voyage* celebration, rather than the traditional gloom-session.

We feel sorry, of course, for those who have loved them and are left behind. But we can comfort them with the certainty that the bonds of love—the most powerful and creative form of thought—are eternal and will draw them together with those they have loved in the next existence as we shall see shortly. As Arthur Balfour put it: 'Death cannot long cheat us of love.'[1]

If we have 'something on our conscience', as most of us

have, we need not take ecclesiastical promises of punishment and 'judgement' too gloomily. For if, as suggested earlier, we make our own hells it follows that *we can also unmake them* for which, no doubt, there will be ample opportunity. And, with the processes of thought operating automatically to keep a check on human error, it is hard to see any need at all for heavenly Courts of Justice or for indeterminate sentences to Cosmic Penitentiaries.

3

As there are two questions about death that trouble some people, perhaps we should try to find the answers:

Many fear that death will be a lonely journey. This fear, surely, overlooks Nature's perfect organization and underestimates her forethought. As she normally makes marvellous arrangements to look after new arrivals on this planet—whether human babies or young animals—we can safely assume that she makes similar provision for new arrivals in the next existence.

We can only guess, of course, what that is. It is often reported that dying people see dead relatives or friends hovering around—Sir Auckland Geddes, for instance, once reported the interesting experience of a man who nearly died.[2] These things, of course, cannot be proved and the reported visions of the dying may be hallucinations. On the other hand, it may well be part of Nature's organization to provide a 'reception committee' of former relatives or friends to ease the transition from this existence to the next.

Whatever Nature's arrangements may be, doctors and nurses who have attended many deathbeds report that those who know that they are dying rarely display any sense of fear.

Another question that bothers some is how they will find former relations or friends in the next existence. A 'reception committee' may be the answer. But, if there is no such thing, Professor Vasiliev's researches offer a clue because, it will be remembered, he found that the thoughts of a hypnotist can reach the mind of the percipient, if the former merely holds a picture of the latter; and that it is not necessary for the hypnotist to know where the percipient is.

As neither time nor distance affect the 'telecommunication' system, discussed in the last chapter, our thoughts will be able instantly to reach those of whom we have a mental picture, though we have no idea where they are. No doubt this can happen while we are dying—or if we think we are likely to die—and in this way dead relations and friends can be made aware that we may be about to join them. This could explain how the 'reception committees'—if they exist —are summoned to the deathbed.

This raises the question of communication between the living and the dead. There is impressive evidence that this is sometimes possible and the writer has known personally men of high intelligence and complete mental stability who have been convinced that it is. These included such men as the eminent scientist, Sir Oliver Lodge and Sir Arthur Conan Doyle, creator of Sherlock Holmes, who took this reporter —on a newspaper assignment—to visit most of the leading mediums of those days.

Whether or not communication with the dead is sometimes possible, the writer can suggest three reasons why it is most undesirable to attempt it, except at the point of death or for purposes of scientific inquiry. The first is that the risks of error, self-delusion and disappointment are extremely high, even with honest mediums, because the wishes, thoughts and memories of the inquirer, telepathically picked up by the medium, may easily be mistaken for messages from the dead.

The second reason is that the emotions of the inquirer may lay him or her wide open to fraud and even robbery by dishonest mediums, some of whom know conjuring tricks which are hard for the novice to detect.

The third reason is that it seems egotistical, inconsiderate and plain bad manners to try to bother those in the next existence with the sorrows and problems of this one because, it is to be hoped, they have more interesting and important things to think about. To try to pester dead relations with one's own worries seems worse than bothering friends on vacation with unnecessary business phone-calls.

4

As everyone knows, death must come to all; and our transition from this existence to another is an important event for us and for those we leave behind. But this natural and inevitable process has been surrounded with such a morbid atmosphere of gloom, fear and mystery that it is often considered in bad taste even to discuss it. And, so intense are feelings about death, that many otherwise-sensible people cannot bring themselves, as we know, to face the inevitable and to make suitable provision for their families; they die intestate, with serious loss to those for whom they would have liked to provide but with immense profit to the legal industry.

This reporter, however, makes no apology for this discussion of death. In this age, more than in any other, it is important to try to look at death in proper perspective because we always have to face the chance of nuclear destruction. Traditional, over-dramatized ideas of death not only add needlessly to the fear of millions but also make us more vulnerable to nuclear blackmail by enemies who do not dread the mass-destruction of human life as much as we do.

Nuclear destruction would merely advance the date of our inevitable transfer to another—and probably more interesting—University, as we have already suggested. For the lucky ones this transfer would be quick and painless; others, it is true, might suffer a slow and painful death, just as many do anyway from various causes such as cancer or automobile accidents.

We can see Patrick Henry's famous declaration: '... give me liberty, or give me death' in a new perspective; the next existence is likely to be far preferable to a life on this planet dominated by gauleiters or commissars—or even bureaucrats.

We need not take too seriously horror-stories about the effects of nuclear fall-out on those who survive because, as we have seen, all the protein in the body is renewed every six months. Anyone, therefore, who does not receive a dose of fall-out too strong for the body to handle is likely to be as good as new after six months. There is no reason to think that fall-out can prevent an L-field from repairing damage if it has not gone too far.

This is confirmed by the experience of Dr. Alvin C. Graves who, with a colleague, accidentally received a heavy dose of radio-activity at the Los Alamos Laboratory. His colleague received more than he did—too much for his body to over-come—and died as the result. Dr. Graves, however, though very sick for six months, recovered and was the father of healthy children.[3]

Excessive fear of nuclear attack, therefore, is not only unjustified but also folly because it may encourage our enemies.

All this, by the way, is an answer to those of the younger generation who use the threat of nuclear destruction as an excuse to dodge the 'courses' of the University of Earth.

5

Next to birth and death, marriage is usually the most important event in the lives of most of us. Can anything we have found shed any new light on this well-worn, over-written subject? Yes—we can get a new perspective on two kinds of love—the mutual attraction of two personalities and physical attraction. And, though these often go together, it is easier to examine them separately.

Of the two, the former is best exemplified by that delight-ful phenomenon, 'love at first sight' of which poets have sung and which was the theme of that famous song from 'South Pacific', *Some Enchanted Evening*. This is the kind of love that yields an indissoluble lifetime companionship of ever-increasing mutual affection.

Though it may seem unromantic to say so, 'love at first sight', in most cases at least, is probably instant, subconscious *recognition*, because the boy and the girl have had some close and affectionate association in a previous existence, whether on this planet or elsewhere. Consciously they remember nothing of this but it is all stored in the 'freezer compart-ments' of their permanent memories; and when their thought-fields interact and scan each other, their 'mental radars' send back a recognition-signal—a kind of I.F.F.* of love.

Their previous relationship need not necessarily have been husband and wife, especially if they knew each other in some non-human existence, where—as Christ said—'there is no giving in marriage'. If they knew each other in some previous life on earth, they could have been mother and son, father and daughter or brother and sister.

For some rare and fortunate couples, mutual recognition is instantaneous and complete. More often, as the girl is usually more intuitive than the boy, she is likely to get a swifter and stronger 'recognition-signal' than he does. But her charm—enhanced by the sudden realization of love—can soon help him to catch up with her—provided that she is careful not to scare him.

Recognition, of course, is not the only kind of love between two entities and, in fact, is probably relatively uncommon. A couple can get favourable 'I.F.F. signals' from each other without any previous acquaintance because they have mutually-compatible personalities. It may take them longer, however, to realize this than the lucky people who have known each other before.

Mutual attraction between two personalities is obviously an individual, non-physical thing which may have nothing to do with physical attraction or sex; as we know, it can be the basis of strong friendships between men and men or women and women as well as between men and women. Physical attraction, on the other hand—Nature's bait to perpetuate the race—is less individual and specific, as any healthy man or woman realizes.

As we all know how much trouble physical attraction can cause, there is no need to elaborate. But there is one aspect of it which will be news to psychologists and marriage counsellors—the part played by the L-fields:

Just as two T-fields—or entities—can be compatible emotionally, so can two L-fields be compatible electronically. But there is an important and dangerous difference: *while*

* Identification Friend or Foe. Equipment, originally invented by the British, which—when triggered by the scanning of friendly radar stations —sends back a coded recognition-signal.

*the attraction between T-fields or entities is usually perman-
ent, the attraction between L-fields can and does fluctuate.*

Voltage-gradients in the human L-field are not constant but
vary over periods of days and weeks in a series of interlocking
cycles—as we noted in an earlier chapter. It is obvious, therefore, that there are times when the L-fields, of a boy or a
girl will be more mutually-attractive—for purely electronic
reasons—than at others. And, as the L-fields extend beyond
the surface of the body, they can react with the L-fields of
others in close proximity.

More research on this fascinating phenomenon must be
done before it is fully understood. But a friend of the writer's
has carried out experiments which indicate that the voltage-
gradients of our L-fields are certainly one of the factors in
physical attraction. He has observed, in fact, that if a red-
blooded boy happens to meet a healthy girl when the two
L-fields are at a complementary 'peak' it is difficult to restrain
them from leaping into bed together.

This phenomenon can explain those sudden, violent and
often-disastrous infatuations of which most of us have known
examples. It can also explain a common occurrence: a boy
may find a girl unusually attractive one day and, two weeks
later when he meets her again, will wonder what he ever saw
in her. The explanation is that the voltage-gradients have
changed their phases in the interval and are no longer so
compatible.

Unfortunately, as we all know, physical attraction can be so
strong—whatever the state of the L-fields—that it can black-
out our 'I.F.F.' equipment. For this, of course, can not only
detect a friend; it can also warn us of a hostile or incompatible
personality, if we give it time and the opportunity to function
without the over-riding interference of physical attraction.

It is just possible that all this may help some anxious
parents to convince the young that there are two kinds of
'love' and to persuade them, when they think themselves in
love, to allow a reasonable cooling off period before they
shackle themselves with marriage. For, apart from the
obvious advantages of being cautious, time may allow their
'I.F.F.s' to overcome the interference of physical attraction
and also may give their L-fields a chance to find their *average*

working-level. That a starry-eyed couple, however, would be willing to listen to this scientific approach to love seems distinctly improbable.

6

We have already found some reasons for thinking that we are products of our past—whether we spent it in human form or otherwise—and so are responsible for our present state. We have also found that the organization of the Universe cannot tolerate any accidents, even if it sometimes seems to us that it does. But it is worth taking a further look at these conclusions because if we can be quite certain that there is no such thing as an 'accident of birth' we can gain a new perspective on some problems of these times.

Since organization—the basic 'ingredient' of everything—is the direct opposite of chance, a *perfect* organization cannot allow itself to be contaminated by *any* elements of chance because, if it did, it would not be a perfect organization. This, of course, does not preclude change; but all change must be controlled by precise laws of cause and effect, in which chance plays no part, even if we do not understand what those laws are.

Even Heisenberg's famous 'uncertainty principle' cannot be an exception to this rule. It states that certain pairs of quantities cannot both be simultaneously determined with unlimited accuracy. But all this means is that it is beyond the power of *human* knowledge and instruments to do so—not that it is beyond the capacity of an omniscient Essence.

Nor does the freewill which Nature has given us violate this rule. This is because a perfect organization implies—*and requires*—complete foreknowledge of how freewill will be used. If it could not foresee and provide for all contingencies things would soon go haywire.

This does not restrict freewill; and a simple analogy may help to show why: Suppose a father takes his child to a toy-store and tells him he can buy anything he likes. If the father has a *complete* knowledge not only of his child's desires but also of all the stock in the store, he will know in advance what the child will buy and how he will use it—without in any way restricting his freedom of choice. And if he knows that the child will choose a ball he will foresee the consequences and warn his wife to put away her treasures before the child comes home. Thus the child has enjoyed freewill while accidents to the best china have been averted.

No doubt the freewill that Nature allows us for her great experiment is organized on similar but infinitely more complicated lines. And in any case, it is limited by our own ability, intelligence, character and inclinations as well as by the opportunities which are the consequences of our past.

There is no reason, then, to think that the freewill we enjoy conflicts with our conclusion that the organization of the Universe cannot tolerate any accidents and cannot include any elements of chance. It follows that it is not chance that A is born in better circumstances and with greater opportunities than B, but that this is the result of precise laws of cause and effect. In other words the advantages or handicaps with which we start life on this planet are the result of what we have done—or not done—in our previous existence.

Our parents, our physical heredity, our home environment, the colour of our skins, our race, our nationality, our qualities of head and heart—all these constitute the equipment we need or deserve for the present course in the University of Earth. Marcus Aurelius put it much better in the quotation at the head of this chapter.

Just how the 'circumstances ordered ... in the way of destiny' are organized we do not know. They may be the purely automatic consequences of our past actions or inactions—we ourselves may create our initial advantages or disadvantages in this life in much the same way as we create our 'heavens' or 'hells' in the next. Or there may be some equivalent of a Director of Studies to advise us and to administer the laws of cause and effect. But we can only speculate.

Do we have any choice of our parents before we are born? Or are we automatically attracted, so to speak, to parents who can provide the kind of upbringing we need for our stage of development? We have no clues to the answers to these questions. But it is at least possible that the young who complain that they 'did not ask to be born' or did not choose their parents did, in fact, have some choice. All that seems certain is that parents have no conscious choice of their children and have no idea of what kind of child they will draw out of the grab-bag of eternity. But, however it may be done, we can be sure that it is perfectly organized and that both children and parents get what is best for them at their state of development.

If we do not agree that we are products of our past, our only alternative is to assume that the Creator of the Universe is a slightly-disorganized and capricious tyrant enjoying sadistic amusement from human misfortune. And then we have to explain why the Supreme Intelligence, with all the Universe to play with, cannot find better forms of entertainment.

If we can accept that we ourselves are responsible for our present state we can enjoy two immediate benefits: *we can see that it is foolish to torment ourselves with envy of those more fortunate and also with feelings of guilt about those less fortunate.* We have only ourselves to blame for our own handicaps in life and we are in no way to blame for the handicaps of others.

That is not to say, of course, that we should not try to emulate those who are more successful than we are or that we should not do all we can to help those less fortunate. But there is no reason to feel jealous of the former or guilty about the latter.

On the contrary, there is every reason to try to suppress these emotions. For jealousy is a destructive form of thought which, at the least, reduces our efficiency and, at the worst, can do us serious harm; and unjustified feelings of guilt not only needlessly depress us but also are apt to impair our judgement.

With modern communications and mass-media it is all too easy for unscrupulous politicians and propagandists to generate powerfully-destructive thought-fields of jealousy. They can also exploit natural human sympathy by stimulating baseless social 'guilt-complexes'. But there is no need for us to play into their hands by tuning-in, so to speak, to their sordid wavelengths. And the more we can insulate ourselves from these emotions, the more creative and effective we are likely to be in helping to improve conditions.

All through history, as we know, there have always been unscrupulous exploiters of human jealousy and hatred. But in this century the mass-media and the reduced power of the Churches have made their work easier and potentially more dangerous.

No wonder the leaders of the Communist revolution attacked religion as 'the opiate of the people'; they realized that religious faith makes people less discontented with their lot, less envious of their neighbours and less susceptible to the propaganda of hate. For most Churches taught that advantages or disadvantages in life were due to the 'Will of God'—a teaching which many were willing to accept. The catechism of the Church of England, for instance, urged each child to 'do my duty in that state of life unto which it shall please God to call me'. And congregations sang lustily and with apparent conviction the old hymn:

The rich man in his castle,
The poor man at his gate,
God made them, high and lowly,
And ordered their estate.

With the declining influence of the Churches these sentiments are no longer convincing to those who are dazzled by materialistic science or hoodwinked by propagandists promising to iron out some of the inequalities of life. In fact, they would probably seem 'undemocratic' to the many who do not know what the word democracy really means.

Meanwhile, the Churches can do no more than they are doing to reduce jealousy and hatred because they do not consider the possibility of a previous existence. So they cannot explain to a discontented generation that they are the product of a past for which they alone are responsible, that we are all in different stages of the long development of the individual personality and that neither propagandists nor politicians can hope to achieve what Nature herself never attempts.

But that need not prevent *us* from using our conclusions to inoculate ourselves against the dangerous emotional viruses of this age.

7

Our conclusions offer us a new perspective on current theories that bad 'environments' are the chief cause of crime and lawlessness; and that these can be reduced by crash programmes and massive expenditures to improve 'environments'. Such theories are likely to lead to disappointment because, although slums and ghettos are fertile breeding-grounds of crime, the theorists are really confusing cause and effect.

Since there are no accidents of birth, the environment in which we start life is the result of our past and the opportunity or test we need for this stage of our development. In other words, by our actions or inactions in previous existence, we have made our own present environment and, if we wish, we ourselves can unmake it and overcome its handicaps. This is supported by the fact that all through history many have risen above the most hopeless environments while others have failed to appreciate good environments and have destroyed them. To suppose, then, that everything will be sweetness and light if all tough environments are eliminated is equivalent to thinking that if all college examinations were abolished everyone would be able to graduate *cum laude*.

We should do everything feasible, of course, to promote useful employment and to improve living conditions. But we should not delude ourselves by thinking that this will change the characters of criminals and hoodlums overnight. For criminal tendencies are attitudes of *mind*—qualities of the eternal entity—on which temporary *physical* conditions may have little or no effect.

This is demonstrated by the fact that crime has assumed record proportions in an 'age of affluence' in the United States while there is less crime and lawlessness in poorer countries where, by American standards, the environment of millions is appalling. It is also shown by the fact that some of the worst criminals did not suffer from a poor environment. Almost every day we can read in the newspaper of some czar of organized crime, of some large-scale swindler, or narcotics wholesaler, or crook lawyer who had a good home, upbringing and education but who has defrauded less-privileged but completely law-abiding citizens. And in some of the finest familes there are occasional black sheep who have enjoyed the same environment, upbringing and genes as their admirable brothers and sisters.

Most of us who are born into highly-developed industrialized nations probably have a long history of past experience, tests and opportunities—somewhere and in some form—because otherwise we would not be equipped for the opportunities and challenges of modern civilization; and it seems unlikely that Nature would be so unfair or so inept as to allow this. If, despite that long experience, we start this existence with a complete disregard of the rights of others, our attitude is unlikely to undergo a sudden and dramatic change if, say, a benevolent government transfers us from a slum to a 'garden apartment'.

In short, physical environment may sometimes be a factor in crime and lawlessness but the legacy of previous existence is always a much bigger one. And we should take environmental theories with a large grain of salt.

8

For similar reasons we should sprinkle a lot of salt on current theories that many of our present troubles can be cured by more education. We should take a hard look at the propaganda of the education industry which tries to persuade us that an early Utopia is merely a matter of more and better-paid teachers, housed in bigger and better educational 'plants', complete with vast auditoriums most expensively equipped.

Utopia is unlikely to be achieved so easily. For if children are born naturally stupid, discontented or criminally inclined despite long—perhaps very long—experience in previous existence a few years of instruction in the present one cannot be expected to have any startling effects on their minds and attitudes.

Wherever we existed before we were born we must have had *some* 'education' because the purpose of our existence is to learn by experience. We may not have learned to read and write; we may not have learned history; we may not have been subjected to vast overdoses of those perennial favourites, Shakspeare and Dickens. But we must have had some form of mental training and some experience of relations with others. If, in spite of all this, the results are disappointing—if we are born dull or anti-social—that is our fault because we failed to take full advantage of our opportunities in the past and may even have dropped out of our 'courses'.

For this reason, a few years spent absorbing information mainly concerned with this existence are unlikely drastically to change our nature and habits or dramatically to enhance our ability. So if we expect too much from education or regard it as a general panacea for everything that ails us we are doomed to disappointment.

Almost any kind of education, of course, is desirable if—and only if—the individual is able and *willing* to profit by it, which is not always the case. At the least, it can offer him the chance, though not the certainty, of earning a better living; and can make life more interesting. At the best it can stretch and train his mind, rather than his memory alone, which will always be helpful to him in any form of future existence. Sometimes, too, it can build on past experience, locked in the 'freezer compartment' of memory.

We sometimes read of children who find a subject so enthralling that, as the *cliché* has it, 'a whole new world is opened to them'. Probably the fact is that an *old* world, stored in their memories, is suddenly *re*-opened. This seems to happen most dramatically to children with past experience of music or mathematics. When introduced to a piano or violin or to the world of figures, they take to it instinctively like ducks to water—and we have prodigies.

We can see, however, that education is not as important in Nature's scheme as educationists fondly imagine because Nature's main concern is the development of individual character. For this academic education is not necessary and all too often it is not concerned with it. Some of the finest characters this reporter has known had little education and at least one could neither read nor write. But their lack of education did not prevent them from developing exceptionally fine qualities, such as integrity, unselfishness, kindness and courage. And most of them developed a shrewd, tolerant and humorous assessment of men and affairs which is lacking in many a Ph.D.

Some of them must have been lucky in their parents, though these could provide little instruction and only the most modest 'environment'. Though parents can often do more than education to promote Nature's purpose they can do little or nothing if the child's previous experience has not made him receptive to their guidance. This is shown by the difference between children of the same parents; some will turn out well, some badly.

When parents are often powerless to help, we should not expect too much from education, especially in these days when most educational institutions are under pressures which leave the faculty little time for anything but academic instruction. Even if they had time for character development it is doubtful if they would care to tackle it because some discipline is required and discipline is now out of fashion in most educational institutions.

Whatever else they may achieve, then, our vast expenditures on education make little direct contribution to Nature's purpose. They probably never will because character cannot be reduced to percentiles or punched into those handy tabulating-cards which most Deans of Admission now find so essential. Perhaps character development is not the proper function of mass education anyway. But, if it is not, the claims of the educationists to be able to help most human problems —given the money and facilities—seem over-optimistic. For only those who co-operate with Nature can hope to be really effective.

Meanwhile our permissive society seems to be lifting the lid of the 'freezer-compartments' of many of the younger generation to the embarrassment of the educationists. This may explain some of the reported dissatisfaction of the young with the curricula offered.

It was suggested earlier that although few of us can consciously remember *details* of past existence and of what we learned in it, these frozen memories can have a profound subconscious influence. From past experience, therefore, many youngsters may be nudged by their frozen memories and may be feeling subconsciously inspired doubts about some of the things they are taught. Without knowing why, in fact, they may have an uneasy certainty that some parent, pedagogue or pundit is talking through his hat.

This must always have been so. But in the days when parents exerted more discipline, the Churches more influence and teachers more authority such doubts were usually strangled at birth. Children were made to feel unfilial if they questioned parents' opinions, ungodly if they doubted preachers' dogma and peculiar if they did not accept the pronouncements of pedagogues.

As this suppression of honest doubt was often overdone we would expect the pendulum to swing violently the other way in this easy-going age; and the genies of what Joan Grant calls 'far-memory' seem to have been uncorked from innumerable bottles. Within limits this may not be a bad thing because the more the individual can respond to the frozen memories of his past, the easier for him to work with Nature rather than against her, which will help him and those with whom he is associated. Even if this is a partial explanation of the present 'revolt of youth', it will not be much comfort to academic presidents and principals when the rocks are coming through their windows and their offices are being devastated. But no problem can be solved until all its causes are understood; and it may help to find a solution if the possibility that youth is influenced by past experience is at least considered. And this might lead to a fresh understanding of their doubts and a new sympathy with their problems.

This is not to suggest that *all* the present 'revolt of youth' is the result of past experience. Some of it, in fact, may be cleverly inspired and organized by our enemies. 'Student revolts' have been a standard Communist technique for years.

9

All the laws of Nature that we know are inexorable; effect follows cause with relentless, mathematical precision. Nature is not 'permissive' and, if she were available for censure, no

doubt she would be denounced as 'undemocratic' and tyran-
nical by some of our *intelligentsia*. For she ruthlessly
eliminates surplus or defective living forms and even whole
species which do not make the grade in her scheme of things.
Sometimes, too, she drastically reduces the human population
by plagues, floods and other natural disasters.

We have found reasons for thinking that her checks on
human conduct are just as inflexible and operate with automatic precision, though cause may take longer to produce
effect than with some of her other laws—no doubt because
of the freedom she allows us. And we have only to look
around to see that she subjects a large proportion of humanity
to stern tests and harsh disciplines of various kinds.

Although these facts of life are obvious enough, this age
has produced an unusually-copious supply of naïve theorists
who ignore them. We have a bumper crop of muddleheads
who confuse democracy with indiscipline and liberty with
licence. We have coveys of psychiatrists who advise parents
not to discipline their children so as not to 'weaken their
egos'—a piece of nonsense which raises belly-laughs among
graduates of West Point or Annapolis. We have flocks of
twittering sentimentalists who feel that the criminal is more
important than his victims.

Though, no doubt, they do not realize it, such theorists
are really claiming to know better than Nature; if Nature
does not hesitate occasionally to chasten the human race and
also to eliminate anything that does not suit her purpose, we
need not be afraid to exert discipline and to punish or
imprison those who do not conform with our laws.

Theories to the contrary, however, make a strong appeal
to those who are lazy, unsure of themselves or lacking in
moral courage because to discipline children is always tedious,
hard work and often distressing; and to punish a criminal
often a painful duty. So it is simple for the theorists to persuade the tenderhearted and gullible that the easiest and
least painful course is the best one—and one compatible
with the highest ideals.

Whatever they profess, their motives are not always altruis-
tic because, by a happy coincidence, these theories can often
be profitable. Unscrupulous psychiatrists, for instance, can

make a good living by 'treating' children who would do better with a little parental love and discipline. As a result, children are launched into a harsh world, quite unprepared for the discipline that life imposes.

Many criminal defence lawyers in the United States persuade an unthinking public and acquiescent judges that to employ every legal trick and gimmick to delay trials is to promote the highest standards of justice and to give the criminal every chance. They do not mention, however, that for every week, month or year they can keep their client out of jail on bail they can exact fees, often paid out of the clients' ill-gotten loot. This racket encourages crime because most authorities agree that the swifter the justice, the greater the deterrent.

These are merely two examples of the unfortunate results of modern theories which conflict with Nature's practice—disturbed children and a record crime-wave. The application of criminal justice in the United States offers a specially odious comparison with Nature; while her laws operate with automatic exactitude American criminal laws so often function with uncertain turpitude.

Americans pride themselves on the 'rule of law' when, in reality, they are subject to the rule of lawyers—quite a different thing. So, despite—or perhaps because of—a vast over-production of lawyers, they suffer from increasing lawlessness.

10

There are many other things on which we can gain a new perspective from what we have found:

If, for example, bad health prevents us from getting the most out of life we can remember that this is a purely temporary condition—quite insignificant in eternity. In future non-physical forms we shall be free of all restrictions of the body, including its limited range of movement; transportation in space should be no problem. If we return to earth we can hope for a healthier body as the result of what we have learned this time.

Meanwhile, we can cheer ourselves with the thought that

all the protein in the body is renewed every six months and the body's capacity for regeneration is amazingly high. We can assist that process by being as optimistic as possible because, as we have seen, the T-field of the mind can influence the body, for better or worse, through the L-field.

If we feel depressed or frustrated because most of the things we have to do seem futile we can remember that everything we do, however dreary, is part of our course in the University of Earth, like the many things we have to learn at school or college which do not interest us. Similarly, for athletics, we willingly go through long and tedious training—the same old routine day after day—knowing that one day this will pay off. If we look on the 'pointless' things we have to do in our present existence in the same way they can seem less depressing.

At school or college we do not waste time and energy hating our examiners—often we do not know who they are. We accept them as instruments of the system who are doing their job of testing us. If we can think of those who harm us or cause us trouble in the same sort of way—as an inevitable part of our college course—we need not waste energy on hate or hostility which, anyway, may hurt us—'psychosomatically'—far more than them. This, of course, is much easier said than done, when some S.O.B. has pulled a fast one.

Nor need we waste time and energy 'getting our own back'. Why bother with revenge when Nature's checks and balances will eventually do the job much better? This does not mean, of course, that we should always turn the other cheek and let the S.O.B. get away with it. If, without too much trouble, we can make him regret his actions and even make amends that will not only be good for him but may prevent him from playing a dirty trick on someone else—one less able to defend himself. But, if we cannot do anything about it, as is often the case, there is no need for us to lose sleep when we can be certain that Nature will deal faithfully with him in due course.

If we feel inadequate or inferior because some minor tycoon we know seems so much more successful than we are, we can comfort ourselves with the reflection that standards of 'success' in eternity are unlikely to be the same as those of Madison Avenue or Wall Street. In the long run and in other existences we may be better qualified for 'success' than the tycoon.

In any case, we can be certain that our present circumstances and problems are best *for us*. What is good for the tycoon might well be bad for us because each of us needs a different kind of experience. And if only we could know the tycoon's secret problems, which, probably, material success cannot solve, we might realize that we are far luckier than he is.

A feeling of inadequacy is often the result of impatience and of the prevailing belief that we only have 'only one life to live' and must get or achieve all we want before it is over. When we realize that we have all eternity to do anything we want we can feel less impatient—and less inadequate. That feeling, of course, should not be used as an excuse for laziness or for not trying to do our best but it can be an antidote to frustration.

These ideas, naturally, are far easier to state than to put into practice as working convictions. But if, gradually, we can make them the basis of our outlook we can be both happier and healthier.

These, then, are some of the new perspectives we can enjoy, if we can accept the things we have found along the trail we have explored. It has not been a mere academic exercise; if we are willing to use our findings, they have immediate practical applications.

CHAPTER TEN

The Infinite Horizons

Per ardua ad astra
—Motto of the Royal Air Force

1

During the past century there have been some classic examples of the impact of ideas—some striking proofs that thought is a force in its own right, with an immense potential for good or ill:

Darwin's Theory undermined the dogma and damaged the age-old influence of the Christian Churches. The theories of Karl Marx and Adolf Hitler changed the course of history. And there have been some economic theories of which the final world-wide effects still remain to be seen.

When a theory or idea is expounded it sets up a T-field which, if conditions are right, may arouse sympathetic 'oscillations' in the minds of millions, just as a small pebble can cause ripples in the largest pond. As suggested earlier, in the realm of thought, like attracts like and a T-field will only get a response from those minds which are, so to speak, on the same wave length of thought, just as a radio transmitter will only affect those receivers which are tuned to the same frequency.

We can safely assume, for instance, that the T-field set up by Darwin did not cause the mind of the then Archbishop of Canterbury to oscillate sympathetically, even if he took the time to study the Theory. It is improbable, too, that the theories of Karl Marx would have evoked any sympathy from the Governor of the Bank of England of those days if he had happened to hear about them. And we all know that the theories of Adolf Hitler were not taken seriously by most people *outside* Germany—until it was too late.

For T-fields to have their *maximum* impact, not only must there be many minds on the same 'wave length' but, also, other conditions must be right. Darwin's Theory, for example, would probably have been less well-received if it had been expounded a century before the industrial revolution and the beginnings of modern science. Imperial Russia's incompetent leadership and disastrous losses in World War I—and the hardships of the peasants—helped to fertilize the soil for Marxist ideas. In Germany, the consequences of defeat in World War I and the megalomania of the militarists helped to make Nazism possible.

In Russia and Germany, too, the ideas of the Communists and Nazis were backed—and all resistance to them suppressed—by ruthless force. But in both cases, the *initial* cause was a T-field set up, oddly enough, by an obscure individual who would have won no prizes for lucid expression, still less for personal charm or, in the modern jargon, 'charisma'.

As a refreshing contrast, Sir Winston Churchill—a prominent personality and a master of English—generated force-fields of thought of quite a different kind. These were creative, appealed to the universal desire for freedom, and so were in harmony with Nature's plan. In President Kennedy's brilliant phrase, Sir Winston 'mobilized the English language and sent it into battle', armed with deadly arrows of humour, against which his humourless enemies had no defence. By the T-fields he set up—and also by his personal example—he generated in his countrymen indomitable forces of courageous thought which—by a narrow margin—saved his country from defeat, and the world from disaster.

Here again, conditions were right for T-fields to set up a memorable oscillation in the minds of millions. The British people were united in their determination not to be defeated, were eager for courageous leadership, and willing to forget personal differences and to sacrifice life itself for the common cause. So—to use an electronic analogy—there was not only an irresistible oscillation of thought, but also a powerful 'feedback' to sustain and encourage Sir Winston and his colleagues.

One is tempted to paraphrase him and to suggest that 'never in the course of human history has so much been owed by so many to so few *thoughts.'*

These examples of the power of ideas or thought, of which words are the vehicle, should not surprise us because Mind is the basis of everything, as we found in Chapter 8. So we would expect even the puny thoughts and ideas of man— of the same nature as those of the Universal Mind—to be able to produce powerful effects when conditions are right, even if they are badly expressed or perverted by human error or ambition.

2

These dramatic examples of the powers of thought as a force seem to have made little impression on most of the leaders, philosophers and intellectuals of the West, perhaps because Science has assured them that there is no such thing as thought-transmission and that thought is a purely electro-chemical process.

Our enemies, however, are not so naïve; their propaganda and brainwashing techniques are sufficient evidence that they are fully aware of the powers of thought. It has been reported* too, that they are currently spending large sums on para-psychological research.

Strangely enough, the resources of the human mind or 'spirit' always seem to have been appreciated more clearly by military leaders than by philosophers or intellectuals:

'*A la guerre,*' said Napoleon, for instance, '*les trois parts sont les affaires morales.*'

'The true defence of a nation can be found in its own soul,' said General Eisenhower.[1]

'The problem,' said General MacArthur, at the Japanese surrender in 1945, 'is basically theological and involves a spiritual recrudescence.... It must be of the spirit if we are to save the flesh.'

Today, many of the Top Brass of the Armed Forces on both sides of the Atlantic are equally aware of the *military* significance of *les affaires morales* and of the resources of the human spirit.

* See *Psychic Discoveries Behind the Iron Curtain* by Sheila Ostrander and Lynn Schroeder. Englewood Cliffs, N.J.: Prentice Hall, Inc. 1970 and New York: Bantam Books, Inc., 1971.

Though some of our professional intellectuals affect a lofty disdain for 'the military mind', the writer has been amused to observe that 'the military mind' often understands the importance of such intangible qualities of mind as ideas, leadership and morale far better than those who claim to be experts on the cultivation of the mind. He has also noticed, by the way, that the 'military mind' can usually express ideas with greater clarity and force than the 'intellectual' mind. This is lucky because fuzzy orders could lose lives, while academic jargon and ambiguous gobbledegook merely lose attention.

That rare and elusive quality, leadership, is probably the most important intangible with which the Armed Forces must be concerned; and, as it is also important in many aspects of life, it may be useful to examine it in the light of our concept that thought is a force with field properties.

Leadership is not a simple thing but compounded of various attributes. The great leaders of history have usually had great physical vitality and stamina, physical courage, a dominant personality, showmanship, the ability to express themselves forcefully and, most important, an impregnable self-confidence. This essential component of leadership is, of course, non-physical, a quality of mind, or—if you prefer it— a special form of T-field.

As a leader can do nothing without followers, it is obvious that his T-field of self-confidence must include the conviction that his followers can do what he wants and will exert their utmost endeavours. This conviction radiates from him and, since thought can produce effects across space, is communicated to the T-fields of the followers and makes them feel confident of success.

We have found that the T-field of the entity can over-ride the L-field—that a powerful 'will to live' can invigorate the L-field and promote recovery. It follows, then, that when a leader radiates his certainty of success to his followers, he stimulates not only their courage and determination but also their L-fields. As a result, however exhausted they may be, they suddenly find new energy to carry on. In other words, leadership can stimulate physically as well as mentally.

Strange as it may seem, we can find some scientific support

for this analysis of leadership from—of all things—Dr. Rosenthal's experiments with rats mentioned in Chapter 4. It will be remembered that he found—briefly—that the rats performed better if the experimenters *expected* them to do better. In other words, the rats reacted favourably to the confidence—or 'leadership'—of the experimenters.

In some recent—and even more important—research,[2] Dr. Rosenthal has shown that if teachers *expect* their pupils to do well, the latter will do better than students whose teachers have been led to believe that their pupils are slow to learn.

To immunize Dr. Rosenthal against any possible venom from the Scientific Establishment, it should again be emphasized that he is in no way responsible for this writer's interpretations of his research.

All this, by the way, suggests a piquant reflection: With due respect and admiration, it is technically accurate to say that General Montgomery's immortal 'desert rats' reacted to the same kind of T-field—though, of course, a much more powerful one—as did Dr. Rosenthal's laboratory rats! With sublime confidence in himself *and in them,* 'Monty' *expected* his troops to win through to victory—and they did.

3

Great natural leaders are usually in short supply. Even if they are available, too, in democratic countries their scope is often restricted—in peacetime at least—by politics, which has been defined as 'the art of the possible'.

Since thought can produce reversible reactions, intelligent use of this phenomenon can offer at least a partial remedy for this perennial problem of the free nations:

If leaders can stimulate and strengthen their followers, the latter, by a 'feed-back of thought' can do the same for their leaders. They can make their task easier and expand 'the art of the possible'.

This, of course, rarely happens, which is unfortunate because in democratic countries the people are really the leaders. Their elected 'leaders', the politicians, cannot gain power without their votes and often cannot act without their approval. So it is obvious that if we, the people, want to get the best out of our 'followers', the politicians, *we ourselves should try to display some of the qualities of leadership*. We should try to learn from the great leaders of history—and also from Dr. Rosenthal's research.

As great leaders expect their followers to do well, we should try to have more confidence in our elected leaders and *expect* them to do their jobs properly—until we know otherwise. This, at the least, would give them a better chance to solve national and international problems. Though this may be sound in theory, it is admittedly hard to apply the theory in practice—especially if our leaders belong to the other party. But it would be worth trying.

Naturally, we should retain and exercise our right to voice *constructive* criticism—a good leader does not hesitate to tear a strip off an incompetent or, if necessary, to replace him. But we should not abuse the right of free speech. We should not harass our elected leaders with selfish demands, with nitpicking criticism or with petty differences—all good leaders give their chosen subordinates a good deal of rein. We should remember, too, that most of us cannot appreciate their problems and do not have access to their sources of information.

Unfortunately, many of the voters in modern democracies display qualities which are the very opposite of leadership. They tend to expect the worst rather than the best from the politicians. 'Politics', in fact, the mechanism of democracy, is all too often a dirty word; and it is the voters who have made it so by making dubious practices possible and profitable.

Great leaders are always alert to help their followers. Too often, we, the people, expect our 'followers'—the politicians —to help us; we look to them for hand-outs rather than performance. In fact, the difference between one political platform and another these days is often merely a question of how best to buy our votes with our own tax-money.

Free speech is often degraded to a free-for-all of mindless cacophony—in the United States, at least, almost any moron or mountebank can gain access to a microphone and an audience of millions. In all the resulting hotch-potch of conflicting T-fields, it is no wonder that the politicians have to devote so much time to keeping their ears to the ground to catch the barnyard cackles of their masters—a posture which invites our enemies to 'catch them bending'. No wonder, too, that the pollsters do a profitable business, even if it is not always helpful.

These trends have probably gone too far for 'sovereign peoples' ever to be able to exercise those qualities of leadership which *should* go with sovereignty. But one day—perhaps in some emergency—it may at least be possible for most people to stop making things needlessly difficult for those to whom they have delegated their authority.

4

Leadership, of course, is merely one aspect of the vast potential of the force of thought. If misuse of the powers of Mind can cause infinite trouble, constructive use of these powers can open up infinite horizons. If the wrong kind of T-field can cause problems, the right kind can solve them.

Probably the most constructive and helpful T-fields we can generate are <u>confidence</u> and <u>courage</u>.

'Today we need a special kind of courage,' said Queen Elizabeth in a Christmas Day broadcast long ago, 'not the kind needed in battle, but a kind which makes us stand up for everything we know is right, everything that is true and honest. We need the kind of courage that can withstand the subtle corruption of the cynics, so that we can show the world that we are not afraid of the future.'

In his remarkable series of films—'Civilization'—Lord Clark has pointed out that the very existence of civilization depends on confidence in the future. Since confidence and courage are closely allied, we must try to develop that 'special kind of courage' described by Queen Elizabeth, in order to 'show the world that we are not afraid of the future'.

This kind of courage is easier to acquire when we remember that our present existence is merely an episode in eternity and that there is no reason to fear the eternal future, whatever may happen in this brief term in the University of Earth. As President Roosevelt said, 'The only thing we have to fear is fear itself', because fear is a destructive kind of T-field, as the effects of panic have so often demonstrated.

If our civilization depends on confidence in the future, it is obvious that fear will erode it. Fear of what the future may bring will weaken the economy by discouraging the risks and enterprise on which its maintenance and growth depend. Fear of what our enemies might do to us encourages them to be aggressive, just as concessions to a blackmailer encourage him to extort more; to show fear of war—as distinguished from *dislike* of war—makes war more probable. And personal fears not only inhibit creative thinking but also weaken us physically by their effect on our L-fields.

As an antidote, then, to the various forms of fear which are damaging Western civilization, we need to produce 'countermeasures of thought'*—constructive T-fields of courage and confidence in ourselves and our system. Moreover, 'you cannot shoot an idea', and only better ideas will defeat the erroneous ideas which have caused our civilization so much trouble.

Countermeasures of courage and confidence are relatively easy to develop during a 'hot' war or some clear-cut emergency—some natural leaders will usually emerge to stimulate them, as Sir Winston did. It is not so easy, however, to develop countermeasures of thought in a long-drawn-out 'cold' war, or in some economic crisis when possible action is less obvious or is more controversial.

But it can be done if sufficient individuals realize the need and start thinking and talking about it. As proof of what a few individuals can do, we have the present world-wide countermeasures of thought against pollution and in favour of conservation. When the late Rachel Carson and a few other dedicated individuals initiated this T-field, probably not even they would have dared to predict that it would produce such widespread and sympathetic oscillations of thought in such a short time.

This not only shows what can be done, but also what can be done by the people themselves despite the indifference—and even the opposition—of the 'leaders' and the 'experts'. It is a striking demonstration of the fact that new and crea-

---

* This term is suggested by the analogous 'radio-countermeasures' of World War II—electronic wizardry with radio-frequencies which defeated many an enemy plan.

tive ideas often well up from the 'ranks' rather than seep down from the 'generals'.

Countermeasures of thought, then, are our job—not the Governments'. There is no need to establish, say, an Agency for Thought Development and Administration (A.T.D.A.) in Washington, or a Standing Committee on Thought (under the chairmanship of the Lord Privy Seal) in Whitehall—whatever contribution these might make to national hilarity. The very last thing we want is the 'thought-control' by the State of the kind exploited by our enemies and, anyway, bureaucracy is one of the most effective contraceptives of new ideas.

Nor do we need any of those enormous, 100 per cent-air-conditioned 'research-centres' with 'fully-landscaped recreation areas', bulging with men and women with more degrees than imagination. And we certainly do not need any new religious movement because our aim is to find as many things as possible on which people of different views and faiths can agree.

Countermeasures of thought are a job for everyone who values individual freedom and our free civilization, and is willing to make a little effort to preserve both. And the more people who make the effort, the sooner the job will be done, our present risks reduced, and our problems on the way to solution.

5

In simple terms, *our job is to strengthen our own morale and to clarify, fortify and unify our own thinking and ideas* as far as possible, so that we can present and exemplify them with greater force and conviction. As the late Adlai E. Stevenson once warned us,[3] we need 'to rediscover the real purpose and direction of our existence'.

'In a free society,' he went on to say, 'there is no alternative but to tap the vigor, faith and imagination of the people themselves. *We must find out once more who we are.*' (Our italics.)

To re-examine our own ideas, 'to rediscover the real purpose and direction of our existence', may not be so easy or so glamorous as dealing with some tangible emergency. But we cannot escape the fact that our present emergency is mainly the result of intangibles—of the perverted ideas of the enemies of Western civilization, of the steady erosion of our ideals and of the confusion of our ideas. And intangibles can only be countered by intangibles, whether we like it or not.

Unless we in the West have all been crazy for a long time, there is nothing basically wrong with our ideals and beliefs. But the easy victories of Communism in 'the Battle for Men's Minds' show that *there is something wrong with us*. In meeting the ideological challenge of fanatical enemies with their assorted '-isms', we of the freeworld can neither exemplify nor express our ideals with sufficient force and conviction. Our countermeasures of thought have been blunted or non-existent.

But if, today, we can promote the conversation of our resources, surely we can advance the conservation of our ideals?

We in the West do not lack physical courage—as two World Wars have shown. But our moral courage is not always able to 'withstand the subtle corruption of the cynics'—in Queen Elizabeth's phrase—or of the materialists or of the 'yes-but-ers' who try to qualify or befuddle even the obvious.

Our moral courage, too, and our belief in ourselves is not always proof against insidious propaganda from our enemies. They probably do not question our physical courage but—acutely aware of the power of ideas—are always probing for weaknesses in our moral courage and stamina. They are encouraged to push us around if we give the impression that these qualities are lacking.

In meeting this challenge by developing countermeasures of thought, we have one great advantage over our enemies:

In the preceding pages we have seen that modern research can now offer some factual and rational support for our basic beliefs. We have found evidence that Nature attaches great importance to the human individual and also to his freedom because, without freedom, he cannot properly fulfill the purpose of his existence, which is to develop by experience. We can fortify ourselves with the certainty that freedom is a natural law, which man violates at his peril. We know that those who promote freedom are working with Nature, and that those who would restrict it are working against her—and must eventually face the consequences. We know, too, our part in Nature's plan and our limitless destiny.

By contrast, totalitarian and other notions which would restrict the freedom of the individual are based merely on theory, wishful thinking, or personal ambition. Such concepts can never be more than a matter of belief while to us the concept of freedom can be a certainty.

No doubt we can find much more support for the beliefs and ideals of the West, if we look for it. With all the resources of modern knowledge and scholarship, we should explore every possible *new* approach to the eternal verities. We should search for every scrap of evidence to make them as obvious and convincing as possible to as many people as possible. For the more facts and reasons we can find to back our ideals and convictions, the sooner our countermeasures of thought will eliminate the ideological infections which have done so much harm to the human race.

Though this, of course, will take a little time, we can reap immediate benefits from developing more of 'that special kind of courage'. As soon as our enemies realize that we in the West have developed a new resistance to bluffs, threats and propaganda, they will be more reluctant to start new wars and more anxious to terminate old ones. We ourselves—fortified by new courage and confidence—should gain a new sense of vigour and purpose and a greater ability to solve new problems. We should also feel better physically because our new optimism should strengthen our bodies through our L-fields.

Economic problems, too, will be easier to solve because that elusive intangible, confidence, plays a great part in economics. In fact, the solution of many economic problems depends more on human attitudes than most professional economists seem to realize. That current and obstinate problem, inflation, for instance, is largely caused by two intangibles—plain greed and the lack of a sense of obligation to give full value for money received.

6

Since Mind and organization underlie everything that exists, we can set no limits to the powers of Mind. In theory, then, the human mind—a reflection of the Universal Mind—should ultimately be capable of any attainment. In practice, however, while it is associated with a human body and subject to the conditions of this planet, there must be a definite 'ceiling' to possible achievement, though we can have no idea how high it may be. In future existences, however, when we are no longer restricted by the dense matter of Earth, the possibilities seem unlimited.

Meanwhile, even in this existence on this planet, there is probably far greater scope for the constructive use of the powers of mind than we can at present imagine. Modern research shows that thought has field properties and can exert its effects across space, without regard to time or distance. It has shown that the T-fields set up by one person can influence the T-fields of others. It has shown that thought has measurable effects on the human L-field.

This, surely, opens up vast new territories to explore and offers great opportunities for creative research, which could have beneficial effects on many aspects of human existence and endeavour. The door is now open, in fact, to the science of the future.

Since the beginning of this century, we have perfected means rapidly to disseminate thoughts and ideas to most of the inhabitants of this planet. But we have not perfected—and have rarely considered—the best ways to use these technical achievements for the good of humanity. We have devised marvellous guns, so to speak, without bothering to find the best ammunition.

This is not to suggest, of course, that we should use modern means of communication for 'propaganda' in the accepted sense. But we should be able to find constructive ideas to disseminate which would reduce world tensions and animosities. If removal of worry can heal ulcers in the body, perhaps a general reduction of anxiety could heal ulcers in the body-politic of nations.

It would be foolish to imagine that this would be easy. But surely it is not beyond the imagination and intellectual capacity of the West? And in view of the disastrous effects of ideas which we have witnessed since the beginning of this century, surely it is at least worthwhile to *try* to devise counter-measures of thought?

This, in fact, may well be the greatest opportunity—and the toughest test—that Nature has ever offered to the students of the University of Earth. And perhaps the whole future of the University depends on the outcome.

7

Per ardua ad astra. This proud motto of the Royal Air Force —so often and so gallantly exemplified—sums up the whole adventure of life for all of us.

Most of us have never had any doubts about the *ardua.* But, along the trail we have explored, we have found reasons to be certain that they lead us to the stars.

Moreover, we have found good reasons to take a more hopeful and encouraging view of the *ardua* of life:

We have found that there is no human situation that cannot be alleviated by the knowledge that it is an essential but temporary experience—a mere incident in our eternal adventure.

We have found that there is no human problem that cannot be transformed by the opportunities of eternity.

With Nature's faultless organization, and with all eternity for it to function—with the great potential of the human mind—there is no legitimate ambition that cannot eventually be achieved, no proper interest that cannot be gratified. There is no limit to future happiness and interest.

There is no human relationship that cannot be mended, no friendship that cannot be re-cultivated, no love that cannot be requited or fulfilled, no pang of bereavement that cannot be healed by a joyous reunion. For our endless adventure knows no bounds of time, of space, or of opportunity.

By the magic alchemy of Nature's plan there is no human experience, however harsh or tragic, that may not be transmuted to the fine gold of evolved wisdom, no wounds of the soul that cannot be changed to stronger sinews of the spirit, if we but look for the opportunity in every difficulty.

'My marks and scars I carry with me,' said Bunyan's Mr. Valiant-for-Truth, as he went down to the river, 'to be a witness for me, that I have fought his battles, who now will be my rewarder.' So the marks and scars of the spirit that we gather in the adventure of human life are evidence that the entity has grown in strength and wisdom.

When we have crossed the river, we shall recognize the chastisements of life for what they are. Stern Nature will be revealed as a kindly schoolmistress of the old type, who hid a sympathetic smile behind a frown as she caned her pupils for the good of their characters and the development of their minds. Then we shall see clearly the benevolent purpose, the perfect justice and the unfailing wonder of our eternal adventure.

These are the certainties with which we can arm ourselves against the dismal theories of our enemies and the no-less-depressing ideas of our home-grown materialists.

8

Since every book must have an end, we can blaze the trail no further; and, appropriately perhaps, these final pages are written at the end of a rough, little-known road, deep in mountainous Canadian forest. Though the road ends here, the forest stretches on, climbing ridge on ridge over the mountain beyond the sight of man. With its promise of further trails to explore, of further adventures of the mind and body, of endless, unguessed horizons stretching upward to the sky, surely the forest is symbolic of the adventure of life?

To walk through it, too, is to find at every turn confirmation of Nature's marvellous designs and kindly, all-embracing forethought. There are the myriad tiny seedlings starting life, protected by the fallen branches of dead trees or crops of wild raspberries. There are the countless, perfectly-formed ferns and the delicately-tinted mosses and lichens, growing in profusion to satisfy Nature's love of variety and beauty. Everywhere there are signs of the interdependence of living forms and of the perfect, ceaseless cycle of decay and replenishment. All around is the varied provender for the creatures of the forest.

Winter is fast approaching and, guided by all-wise Nature, the forest and its creatures are making their final preparations. The solemn spruce and the bright hardwoods, still flaunting the last tatters of their fall finery, have already converted the free water in their cells to chemical forms which will not freeze and disrupt their structure. The deer have withdrawn to the snug depths of the forest now that the orchards of abandoned, bordering farms can no longer offer apples. The little red squirrels have nearly completed their winter hoards of food—and one chittered and swore at this reporter this afternoon for interrupting such serious business.

Long ago, the Canada geese formed their convoy over the forest towards the shore and headed swiftly to far-distant winter haunts, flying in perfect formation and with unerring navigation. But the wild duck are still on the pond, gobbling those special delicacies that Nature provides at this season.

This—and much more—the forest can show us of Nature's forethought and organization. Can anyone who sees it seriously imagine that this is all an accident, without purpose —and without love? Is it possible to believe that man is some mysterious exception, deprived of Nature's benevolence and wisdom?

Is it possible to credit that all this is happening just because, aeons ago, some mindless, aimless atoms met in some fortuitous and wildly-improbable convention?

If the forest is not enough to reassure us, let us walk out and look at the sky in all the crystal brilliance of a Canadian night:

Far above, towards Labrador, the Northern Lights shimmer and scintillate in wanton display of their delicate, unearthly folds and colours. It is as if Nature herself, relaxing from the cares of summer, were dancing a gay but stately measure to the music of the spheres, swirling the skirts of her wondrous raiment.

Almost overhead, the North Star winks to its partners of the Southern Cross far beyond the curve of this whirling globe and, all around it, rank on rank clear across the dome of the heavens, untold myriads of stars and planets keep their long-appointed paths with ageless and perfect accuracy.

Are all this beauty, this majesty, this precision, mere products of chance, without aim, without imagination, without organization?

Our physicists may explain, if they wish, that the Northern

Lights are caused by particles ionized by cosmic rays in the earth's magnetic field, just as manufacturers of paint can tell us that the colours in an artist's masterpiece are caused by light striking particles of pigment embedded in oil. But such dismal information in no way explains the shapely forms of the auroran curtains or the inspiring design of the artist— still less that something in man which responds to beauty in Nature and aspires to know its Cause.

9

Alone in a forest clearing on such a night, even a reporter may be permitted his fancies. . . .

When the moon has completed another cycle it will be nearly Christmas and, looking at the stars, imagination turns to that resplendent Star in the East of the first Christmas long ago. Since nothing in all creation can ever be lost, perhaps that Star still swings on towards the outer reaches of space, far beyond those faint specks of light, a tireless beacon of tidings of great joy for other Christmases in other worlds beyond our ken. Perhaps it has turned the limit of its course and, even now, is once more racing earthwards, one day to light the birth of another Babe, destined to sustain and guide the faltering steps of man.

No man can foretell what wonders the future may hold. But already in this age there has been wonder enough. Already the Wise Men of the West have produced their own star, blazing over another desert, to signal the birth of new knowledge for man—that first revealing atomic flash in the wilds of New Mexico not so many years ago.

No herald angels sang its import. But its message was clear; that blinding light proved beyond all doubting that solid matter is fickle and that it is organization, the Mind of the Creator—of which the mind of man is a spark—which is the ultimate, everlasting reality.

To those with eyes to see, then, that Star in the West can serve this age as a beacon of hope. It can illumine anew those age-old truths, those ancient faiths, by which alone man may advance to the infinite horizons of his eternal destiny.

List of References

Chapter 1

1. Tuchman, Barbara. *The Proud Tower*. New York: The Macmillan Company, 1966. Bantam Books, 1967.

'Such sentiments were among the indirect results of the most fateful voyage since Columbus—Charles Darwin's aboard the *Beagle*. Darwin's findings, in the *Origin of Species*, when applied to human society, supplied the philosophical basis for the theory that war was both inherent in nature and ennobling. War was a conflict in which the stronger, and superior race survived, thus advancing civilization. Germany's thinkers, historians, political and military scientists, working upon the theory with the industry of moles and the tenacity of bulldogs, raised it to a level of national dogma. . . . Darwinism became the White Man's Burden. Imperialism acquired a moral imperative.'

2. For example, see Davenport, Russell W. *The Dignity of Man*. New York: Harper Brothers, 1955 (Harper and Row).

'The phenomenal success of the Soviet propaganda in making tyranny look like democracy, slavery look like freedom, evil look like truth—this extraordinary success cannot be due entirely to the cleverness of Soviet propagandists. It must also be due and equally to a failure on our part to . . . breathe life into what we ourselves believe.

'Eighteenth-century formulations of the rights of free men . . . have been taken for granted, as absolutes that relieve us of the necessity of thinking for ourselves. As a result they have aged. They have slipped back into the eighteenth-century, where they were born; events and ideas have marched on without them. And when we Americans cite them as if they were still living and true, we arouse a profound incredulity. . . .

'The cause of freedom has not been stolen from the American with guns. It has been stolen from him with ideas. And he has found himself powerless to formulate his ideas in any way that

175

can engage the confidence of the people of the world.'

See also Carew Hunt, R. N. *The Theory and Practice of Communism.* New York: Macmillan Co., 1951.

See also de Riencourt, Amaury. *Roof of the World—Tibet, Key to Asia.* New York: Holt Rinehart & Winston. London: Victor Gollancz, 1950.

See also van der Post, Laurens. *Venture to the Interior.* New York: William Morrow and Co., 1951.

3. When a distinguished Darwinist published this admission in an article in a national magazine, this reporter wrote to request permission to quote the statement. The Darwinist refused as was his right; and this reporter has no wish to embarrass Darwin fans by referring the reader to the article, where he could find the statement for himself.

4. Rockefeller, Nelson A. 'Policy and the People', *Foreign Affairs*, Vol. 46, No. 2 (January, 1968).

'What is at issue is nothing less than whether life can be given meaning . . . in an environment which sometimes seems to dwarf the individual. The contemporary uneasiness—especially of our younger generation—reflects rebellion against the emptiness of a life which knows only "practical" problems and material goods and seems to lack a deeper purpose. . . .

'The deepest problem before America, then, is moral or psychological. Since much of the current uneasiness reflects a search less for solutions than for meaning, remedies depend for their effectiveness on the philosophy or values which inspire them. . . .

'Decades of "debunking" and materialism have left the younger generation without adequate moral support in face of the challenge of a revolutionary age.'

5. From an Associated Press Despatch from Warsaw, March 12, 1961.

6. Tillich, Paul. 'The Lost Dimension in Religion', *The Saturday Evening Post* (June 14, 1958). Dr. Tillich also wrote:

'What we need above all and partly have is the radical realization of our predicament, without trying to cover it up by secular or religious ideologies. The revival of religious interest would be a creative power in our culture if it would develop into a movement of search for the lost dimension in depth.' Quoted by permission of *The Saturday Evening Post* © 1958 The Curtis Publishing Co.

7. Velikovsky, Immanuel. *Worlds in Collision*. New York: Doubleday & Company, Inc.

8. Grazia, Alfred de (ed.). *The Velikovsky Affair—The Warfare of Science and Scientism*. Hyde Park, N. Y.: University Books, 1966.

Chapter 2

1. de la Mare, Walter. *Peacock Pie*.

2. Dodds, E. C., M.V.O., M.D., F.R.C.P., F.R.S. 'Protein Structure and Clinical Problems', *British Medical Journal* (December 2, 1950). Quoted by permission of the Editor.

3. Hoagland, Hudson, Director of the Worcester Foundation for Experimental Biology. 'The Elements of Life', *An Outline of Man's Knowledge of the Modern World*. Garden City, N.Y.: Nelson Doubleday, Inc., 1960.

4. *Washington Evening Star*, March 23, 1958.

5. *New York Times Magazine*, December 4, 1949. © 1949 by The New York Times Company. Reprinted by permission.

6. Schoenheimer, Rudolph, M.D. *The Dynamic State of Body Constituents*. Harvard University Press and Oxford University Press, 1942.

7. Walker, Boyd, and Asimov. *Biochemistry and Human Metabolism*. Baltimore: Williams and Wilkins Co., 1957.

8. Burr, H. S. and Northrop, F. S. C. 'The Electrodynamic Theory of Life', *Quarterly Review of Biology*, 10 (1935), 322-333.

9. For a general description of the findings of Dr. Burr and Dr. Ravitz, see *Main Currents in Modern Thought*, which devoted an entire issue to their work, Vol. 19, No. 1, September-October, 1962. Foundation for Integrative Education.

Following is a representative selection of the innumerable publications of Dr. Burr and his associates:

Burr, Harold Saxton, Ph.D. *The Nature of Man and the Meaning of Human Existence.* Chas. C .Thomas, Publisher, 1962.

Burr, H. S. 'The Field Theory in Biology', *The Scientific Monthly*, LXIV, No. 3 (March, 1947).

Burr, H. S. and Northrop, F. S. C. 'Evidence for the Existence of an Electro-dynamic Field in Living Organisms', *Proceedings of the National Academy of Sciences*, Vol. 25, No. 6 (June, 1939), 284-388.

Burr, H. S. 'Measurement of Electrodynamic Fields', *Medical Physics Year Book*, III (1960), 59.

Specific References

10. Burr, H. S. and Musselman, L. K. 'Bio-electric Phenomena Associated with Menstruation', *Yale Journal of Biology and Medicine*, Vol. 9, No. 2, December, 1936.

Burr, H. S., and Langman, Louis. 'Electrometric Timing of Human Ovulation', *American Journal of Obstetrics and Gynaecology* St. Louis. Vol. 44, No. 2, pp. 223-230, August, 1942.

11. Burr, H. S., Hill, R. T. and Allen, Edgar. 'Detection of Ovulation in the Intact Rabbit', *Proc. Society for Experimental Biology and Medicine*. *1935-33*. 109-111.

12. Burr, H. S. Interview with author.

13. Burr, H. S. Interview with author.

14. Burr, H. S. Interview with author.

15. Burr, H. S. and Langman, L. 'Electromagnetic Studies in Women with Malignancy of Cervix Uteri', *Science* 1947, *105*, 209-210.

Burr, H. S. 'Biologic Organization and the Cancer Problem', *Yale Journal of Biology and Medicine*, Vol. 12, No. 3, January, 1940.

16. Ravitz, L. J., Jr. 'How Electricity Measures Hypnosis', *Tomorrow*, Vol. 6, No. 4, pp. 49, 56, Autumn, 1958.

Ravitz, L. J., Jr. 'Application of the Electrodynamic Field Theory in Biology, Psychiatry and Hypnosis', *American Journal of Clinical Hypnosis*, Vol. 1, No. 4, April, 1959.

Ravitz, L. J., Jr. 'History Measurement and Applicability of Periodic Changes in the Electromagnetic Field in Health and Disease', *Annals of the New York Academy of Sciences*, Vol. 98, Art. 4, pp. 144-1201, October 30, 1962.

17. Burr, H. S. 'Moon-Madness', *Yale Journal of Biology and Medicine*, Vol. 16, No. 3, January, 1944.

Burr, H. S. 'Electricity and Life—Phases of Moon Correlated with Life Cycle', *Yale Science Magazine*, 1944 -*18*, 5-6.

Burr, H. S. 'Diurnal Potentials in Maple Tree', *Yale Journal of Biology and Medicine*, 1945, *17*, 727-734.

Burr, H. S. 'Effect of Severe Storm on Electric Properties of a Tree and the Earth', *Science* 1956, *124*, 1204-1205.

18. Burr, H. S., Harvey, S. C. and Taffel, Max. 'Bio-electric Correlates of Wound Healing', *Yale Journal of Biology and Medicine*, 1938, *11*, 104-107.

Burr, H. S., Taffel, Max and Harvey, S. C. 'An Electrometric Study of the Healing Wound in Man', *Yale Journal of Biology and Medicine*, 1940, *12*, 483-485.

19. Ravitz, L. J., Jr. *Ibid.*

20. Burr, H. S. and Nelson, Oliver. 'Growth correlates of Electromotive Forces in Maize Seeds', *Proceedings of National Academy of Science, Vol. 32*, No. 4, 73-84, April, 1946.

21. Burr, H. S. 'Electric Correlates of Pure and Hybrid Strains of Corn', *Proceedings National Academy of Science* 1943, *29*, 163-166.

22. Burr, H. S. 'Field Properties of the Developing Frog's Egg', *Proceedings National Academy of Sciences*, Vol. 27, No. 6, June, 1941, pp. 276-281.

23. Burr, H .S., Lane, C. T. and Nims, L. F. 'A Vacuum-tube

Microvoltmeter for the Measurement of Bio-electric Phenomena', *Yale Journal of Biology and Medicine*, 9: 65-76, 1936.

Burr, H. S. 'Variables in D.C. Measurement', *Yale Journal of Biology and Medicine*, 17: 465-478, 1945.

Burr, H. S. and Mauro, A. 'Millivoltmeters', *Yale Journal of Biology and Medicine*, 21: 249-253, 1949.

24. Burr, H. S. 'Biologic Organization and the Cancer Problem', *Yale Journal of Biology and Medicine*, Vol. 12, No. 3, January, 1940, p. 281.

Chapter 3

1. The writer regrets that he is unable to give credit to the author of this penetrating and delightful verse because he has been unable to trace his name. The verse was found in an old book, which did not quote the source. Perhaps some reader can identify the author?

2. du Noüy, Lecomte. *Human Destiny*. New York: Longmans, Green and Co.

3. Wasserman, G. D., Department of Mathematics, Kings College, Durham, England, 'An Outline of a Field Theory of Organismic Form and Behaviour', *Ciba Foundation Symposium on Extrasensory Perception*. Boston: Little Brown and Co., and London: J. and A. Churchill, 1956.

4. *Saturday Evening Post*, May 2, 1959.
More recently, Dr. Rene Dubos, an eminent micro-biologist at Rockefeller University confirmed M. Rostand's statement:
'The evidence is now overwhelming,' stated Dr. Dubos, 'that man's body and brain have not changed significantly during the past 100,000 years. . . .'
Dubos, Rene, Sandor Rado Lecture at Columbia University's College of Physicians and Surgeons. *Columbia Forum*, Spring, 1969, Vol. XII, No. 1. © 1969 by the Trustees of Columbia University in the City of New York.

5. Cannon, H. Graham, F.R.S. *The Evolution of Living Things*. Manchester University Press, 1958; Charles C. Thomas, Springfield, Ill.; Ryerson Press, Toronto.

6. Strömberg, Gustaf. *The Soul of the Universe*. Philadelphia: David McKay Company, 1948. Quoted by permission of Mrs. Strömberg.

7. *New York Times*, August 27, 1952.

8. Associated Press Report from Chicago. November 26, 1957.

9. Dr. Ralph W. G. Wyckoff. Presidential Address to the American Crystallographic Association, June, 1952.

Chapter 4

1. *New York Times Magazine, Ibid.*

2. In an article in *Neurochemistry*, edited by K. A. C. Elliott, Irvine H. Page, and J. H. Quastel. Charles C. Thomas, Publisher, pp. 458-462. In the same publication—p. 38—there is an interesting reference to the incorporation of radio-active phosphorus into brain nucleic acids. This, in turn, refers to a paper by De Luca, Rossiter, and Strickland. *Journal of Biochemistry—* U.S.A., 55/193. 1953.

3. *Washington Evening Star*, May 1, 1959.

4. (a) Following appeared in the *New York Times*, June 30, 1915:

MIND READER WINS BY FEATS IN COURT

W. Bert Reese Readily Quotes text of Hidden Writings to Judge Rosalsky

NAMES THE BANK ACCOUNT

Tested by Assistant District Attorneys and Freed of Fortune-telling charge

W. Bert Reese, whose 'mind-reading' demonstrations have mystified many scientists including Thomas A. Edison and Dr. William Hanna Thompson, author of *Brain and Personality*, was discharged yesterday by Judge Rosalsky on his appeal from a conviction by Magistrate Barlow of disorderly conduct, under a section dealing with fortune-telling.

Reese convinced Judge Rosalsky, Assistant District Attorneys Bostwick and Flint and two reporters by demonstrations in court that he was not a disorderly person but a man with apparently unusual powers. . . .

Reese was arrested February 26 and found guilty. . . .

When his case came before Judge Rosalsky yesterday on appeal Reese asked permission to demonstrate his abilities in court. He told Judge Rosalsky to write something on each of three pieces of paper and to fold them so that he might not be able to read what had been written. Judge Rosalsky put the papers in different pockets after he had mixed them up so that he could not distinguish them himself. Then Judge Rosalsky produced one of the folded papers and pressed it against Reese's forehead.

'You ask me how much money you have in a certain bank,' Reese said. '$15 is the amount.' Judge Rosalsky admitted the answer was correct and produced the second piece of paper.

'This piece contains the name of one of your old school teachers —Miss O'Connor,' Reese said.

The third question which he read correctly but did not answer was, 'What was the rule in the Shelleys case?'

Reese performed similar demonstrations for the benefit of Mr. Bostwick and Mr. Flint and the reporters. His last feat was to give the maiden name of the mother of one of the reporters. All questions were written on General Sessions stationery which Judge Rosalsky supplied.

'I do not consider you a disorderly person,' Judge Rosalsky said when the demonstrations were finished. 'You are honorably discharged.'

(b) Following appeared in the *Washington Post*, September 26, 1958:

Swindling Charge Dismissed
　　　Mind Reader Tested in Berlin Court Wins Acquittal
　　　by his Performance
By Richard O'Regan
BERLIN, Sept. 25 (AP)—Six spectators in a courtroom in suburban Berlin raised their hands. Yes, they told the judge they were willing to have their minds read by the man on trial.

They wrote six questions and handed them to the bench. The judge turned to Gerhard Belgardt, 39, otherwise known as Hanussen II, Germany's No. 1 Mind reader.

None of the spectators nor the mind reader had been told that they might take part in a mind reading test.

Belgardt was accused of swindling clients in private seances by professing to give news of missing relatives.

The judge: 'What is on the first piece of paper?'

Belgardt: 'The lady is asking about her sister. She is an inch taller, considerably younger and works in a public building.'

The questioner: 'That's right. My sister works as a medical assistant.'

The judge: 'What is on the next paper?'

Belgardt: 'The man has asked about his son. He will come along well in school.'

The man: 'Correct.'

The judge: 'The next questioner is a city detective. What has he written?'

Belgardt: 'He asks about his mother or his grandmother. I have no contact. Either the question is phony or she is dead. The man has suffered long—a concentration camp. Is that correct?'

The detective: 'Correct. I asked about my grandmother. She is dead. I was in a concentration camp.'

Three further questions were asked and Belgardt got the answers relatively right.

The judge dismissed the case declaring 'the accused has a certain validity to his claims as a mind reader'.

Hanussen II, embracing his wife: 'I had foreseen that I would be freed.'

5. Rosenthal, Robert and Fode, Kermit L. 'The Effect of Experimenter Bias on the Performance of the Albino Rat', *Behavioral Science*, Vol. 8, No. 3 (July, 1963).

Rosenthal, Robert and Lawson, Reed. 'A Longitudinal Study of the Effects of Experimenter Bias on the Operation and Learning of Laboratory Rats', *Journal of Psychiatric Research*.

6. Vasiliev, L. L., Professor of Physiology in the University of Leningrad. *Experiments in Mental Suggestion*. First published September 18, 1962 by Leningrad State University on instruction from the Editorial Council of the University of Leningrad. English translation authorized and revised by Professor Vasiliev, Copyright 1963—and published—by Institute for the Study of Mental Images. Now, unfortunately, out of print.

Chapter 5

1. Erickson, Milton H. 'Hypnotic Investigation of Psychosomatic Phenomena', *Psychosomatic Medicine Experimental and*

Clinical Studies, Vol. V, pp. 56-58. Baltimore: Williams and Wilkins Co., 1943.

2. Strosberg, Irwin M., D.M.D. and Vics, Irving, O.D. 'Physiological Changes in the Eye During Hypnosis', *American Journal of Clinical Hypnosis,* Vol. 4, No. 4 (April, 1962). p. 264.

3. Ravitz, Leonard J. 'Application of the Electrodynamic Field Theory in Biology, Psychiatry and Hypnosis', *American Journal of Clinical Hypnosis,* Vol. I, No. 4 (April, 1959).

Ravitz, Leonard J. 'History, Measurement and Applicability of Periodic Changes in the Electromagnetic Field in Health and Disease', *Annals of the New York Academy of Sciences,* Vol. 98, Art. 4, pp. 144-1201.

4. Penfield, Wilder, O.M., C.M.G., Litt.B.M.D., F.R.C.S., Hon. F.R.C.P., F.R.S. 'The Excitable Cortex in Conscious Man', *The Sherrington Lectures.* Liverpool University Press, 1958.

5. *Ibid.*

6. Penfield, Wilder and Roberts, Lamar. *Speech and Brain Mechanisms.* Princeton University Press, 1959.

7. Penfield, Wilder. *Engrams in the Human Brain: Mechanisms of Memory.* Gold Medal Lecture, the Royal Society of Medicine, London, April 4, 1968. Proc. R.S.M. Vol. 61, Aug. 1968.

8. Sherrington, Sir Charles, O.M. *Man on His Nature.* Cambridge University Press, 1951.

9. Lashley, K. S. *Brain Mechanisms and Intelligence.* University of Chicago Press, 1929.

10. Maier, N. R. F., Ph.D. and Schneira, T. C., Sc.D. *Principles of Animal Psychology.* Mc-Graw Hill, 1935.

11. Fukurai, T. *Clairvoyance and Thoughtography* (1913). London: Rider and Co., English Translation, 1931.

12. Eisenbud, Jule. *The World of Ted Serios.* New York: William Morrow and Co., 1967.

Chapter 6

1. Kipling, Rudyard. *The Sack of the Gods*—The Definitive Edition of Rudyard Kipling's Verse. London: Hodder and Stoughton Ltd. Quoted by permission of Mrs. Bambridge.

2. Shelley, Percy Bysshe. *Letters to Elizabeth Hitchener.*

3. Jung, C. G. *Memories, Dreams and Reflections.* London: Collins and Routledge and Kegan Paul, 1963, pp. 123-4.

4. Matt. 6: 12. 'But lay up for yourselves treasures in heaven, where neither moth nor rust doth corrupt, and where thieves do not break through nor steal.'

Chapter 7

1. Cerminara, Gina. *The World Within.* New York: William Sloane Associates, Inc., 1957 and *Many Mansions*, London: Neville Spearman Limited, 1967.

2. Langley, Noel. *Edgar Cayce on Reincarnation.* New York: Paperback Library, Inc., 1967.

3. The Bible and Reincarnation. At no time—as far as this writer knows—did Jesus Christ ever suggest that human birth is the beginning of us. On the contrary, there are indications that His disciples took previous existence for granted. For the Bible contains some suggestive references to it:

'Before I formed thee in the belly I knew thee. . . .' wrote the prophet Jeremiah (1 : 5)—surely a clear reference to pre-existence?

Malachi, who apparently wrote long after the death of the prophet Elijah, prophesied 'Behold I will send Elijah the prophet before the coming of the great and dreadful day of the Lord,' (Malachi 4 : 5), which indicates that he believed that Elijah would reincarnate. This was confirmed by Christ when He said:

'For all the prophets and the law prophesied until John. And if ye will receive it this is Elias, which was for to come. . . .' (Matt. 11 : 13) and 'But I say unto you, That Elias is come already, and they knew him not. . . .' (Matt. 17 : 12).

'This *is* Elias . . .' 'They knew *him* not.' Could there be a more definite statement that John had had a previous existence and that, in one life, he had been Elias?

Previous existence emerges again in the story of the man who had been blind from birth (John 9: 2) when the disciples asked: 'Who did sin, this man, or his parents, that he was born blind?' Jesus answered: 'Neither hath this man sinned, nor his parents; but that the works of God should be manifest in him.'

Obviously the disciples would not have suggested that a man should be blind from birth for his sins, if they had not assumed—as a matter of course—a previous existence in which those sins might have taken place.

Pre-existence, too, is suggested by the story (John 5) of the man lying beside the pool of Bethesda who had had 'an infirmity thirty and eight years' and was so crippled and helpless that he could not get to the pool unaided. It is hard to imagine an incapacitating illness which had lasted thirty-eight years and which could have been the result of 'sin' in that particular life. Yet, when Jesus had healed him, He said: 'Sin no more lest a worse thing come unto thee.'

Other references in the Bible indicate that one life on earth rarely allows time for the consequences of our acts:

'Whatsoever a man soweth that also shall he reap,' said Paul (Gal. 6: 7). 'For he that soweth to his flesh shall of the flesh reap corruption; but he that soweth of the Spirit shall of the spirit reap life everlasting.' Many who 'sow to the flesh' do not 'of the flesh reap corruption' in their present lives, but enjoy a vigorous old age. If Paul is taken literally, then, such people cannot get what they deserve 'in the flesh' without a future incarnation. And the converse of his statement must also be true; that we are 'reaping' now what we have sown in the past.

If one lifetime is too short for the punishment to fit crimes peculiar to earth-life, surely one or more further lives on this planet must be needed to allow the punishment to take effect?

This is supported by two strikingly-similar statements in the Old Testament and the New. In Genesis (9: 6) it is stated: 'Whose sheddeth blood, by man shall his blood be shed.' And Jesus said: 'For all they that take the sword shall perish by the sword.' (Matt. 26: 52). The shedding of blood and the use of swords are customs peculiar to human life on this earth; and we cannot expect blood or swords—material things—in some non-material existence. Yet we know that many who 'take the sword' do not 'perish by the sword' in their present lifetimes; and that not all murderers, those who 'shed blood' are caught and executed. If, then, we accept Christ's statement, it is obvious that those who take the sword or shed blood must have a future existence in human form, in which the punishment can take effect.

This inexorable operation of the law of cause and effect may sometimes account for the violent deaths suffered by seemingly-innocent people, which seem to us so unfair. Perhaps this is what Jesus meant when He said: 'It is impossible but that offences will come: but woe unto him, through whom they come!' (Luke 17:1). In other words, some of the victims of the German or Russian slave-camps themselves may once have maltreated slaves. But that is no excuse for the Germans and Russians.

On this planet we would expect the law to operate through human agencies, and each age seems to provide sufficient murderers and barbarians to serve as its instruments. That is not to say, of course, that all who are murdered are paying the penalty for murdering someone in a previous life: the experience may be necessary for some other reason

There is a suggestive reference to reincarnation in the Book of Revelation (3:12): 'Him that overcometh will I make a pillar in the temple of my God, and he shall go out no more.' Of all the books of the New Testament, Revelation is the most ambiguous. But a reasonable interpretation of 'go out no more', surely, is that once an entity has successfully overcome all the tests and trials of earth life, reincarnation is no longer necessary—as the Oriental philosophers maintain.

The Apocrypha contains a delightful reference to previous existence in the *Wisdom of Solomon* (Chaps. 7 and 8): 'I myself also am mortal man . . . and in my mother's womb was fashioned to be flesh in the time of ten months . . . I was a witty child and had a good spirit. Yea rather, being good, I came into a body undefiled.'

It may be argued that references to pre-existence in the Bible are few and slight. But truth does not depend on repetition. Indeed, the very casualness of the references is an indication that pre-existence and future incarnations seemed perfectly normal and obvious to the writers.

Since entities are all different, wherever they happen to be they must require different circumstances and environment for their future development, just as they do when they are occupying human bodies. So, whatever existence without a body may be like, it cannot be exactly the same for all of us; conditions must be 'tailored' to the state of development of the entity.

Jesus stated this poetically and plainly when He said: 'In my Father's house are many mansions; if it were not so, I would have told you. I go to prepare a place for you. And if I go and prepare a place for you, I will come again and receive you unto myself; that where I am, there ye may be also.' (John 14:2, 3).

To an audience ignorant of all intangibles—except 'spirits,'—how better could He have expressed different conditions in our future existence?

4. Penfield, Wilder, O.M., C.C., M.D., F.R.S. *Engrams in the Human Brain: Mechanisms of Memory.* Gold Medal Lecture, The Royal Society of Medicine, London, April 4, 1968.

5. Stevenson, Ian, M.D. *Twenty Cases Suggestive of Reincarnation.* New York: American Society for Psychical Research. Proc. Vol. xxvi, September, 1966.

6. Some examples are: Cerminara, Gina. *Many Mansions.* Neville Spearman Ltd., 1967; Cerminara, Gina. *The World Within.* New York: William Sloane Associates, 1957; Langley, Noel. *Edgar Cayce on Reincarnation.* New York: Paperback Library, Inc., 1967.

Chapter 8

1. Jeans, Sir James, M.A., D.Sc., Sc.D., LL.D., F.R.S. *The Mysterious Universe.* Cambridge University Press, 1930, p. 148.

2. Evans-Wentz, W. Y., M.A., D.Litt., D.Sc. *Tibetan Yoga and the Secret Doctrine.* Second edition, Oxford University Press, 1958, p. 363.

3. Nahm, Milton, *Selections from the Early Greek Philosophers*, pp. 150-151. New York: Appleton-Century Crofts.

4. Jeans, Sir James, *ibid.*, p. 136.

5. Lodge, Sir Oliver, *Hibbert Journal*, about October, 1921. Quoted in *The Company of Avalon* by F. Bligh Bond, F.R.I.B.A. Oxford: Basil Blackwell, 1924.

Chapter 9

1. Balfour, A. J. Quoted in *The Psalm Sunday Case.* Proc. Soc. for Psychic Research, February, 1960.

2. Geddes, The Right Hon. Sir Auckland, P.C., G.C.M.G., K.C.B., M.D. 'A Voice from the Grandstand', *Edinburgh Medical Journal*, Vol. 44, June, 1937, pp. 365-384.

3. Report in the *Evening Star*, Washington, D. C., March 28, 1957.

Chapter 10

1. Speech to a Joint Session of Congress, 1951.

2. Rosenthal, Robert. *Teacher Expectation and Pupil Learning*. 'The Unstudied Curriculum', Association for Supervision and Curriculum Development, NEA, Washington, D.C., 1970.

3. The first A. Powell Davies Memorial Address, Washington, D.C., January, 1959.